Touching Stones

Sketches & Poems

by
Sara Stoops Robbins

Printed in the United States of America

First Printing, 2016

ISBN-13: 978-1533444745
ISBN-10: 1533444749

Robbins Books
192 Castle Drive
Nokomis, Fl

Cover: Peggy's Cove

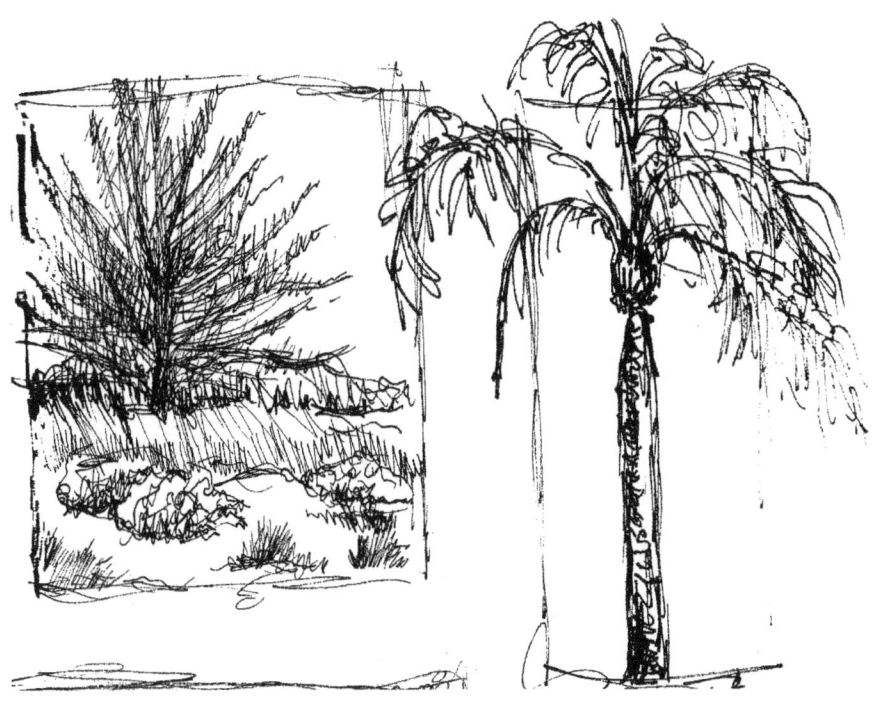

Nokomis, Fl 2014

Acknowledgements and Thanks to

Joel Robbins

> The perpetual wanderer
>
> In mind, spirit and body,
>
> Who patiently dragged me
>
> Along.

Does anyone ever realize life while they live it...every, every minute? Saints and poets maybe...they do some."

Thornton Wilder, Our Town

"A man paints with his brains, and not with his hands."

Michelangelo Buonarroti

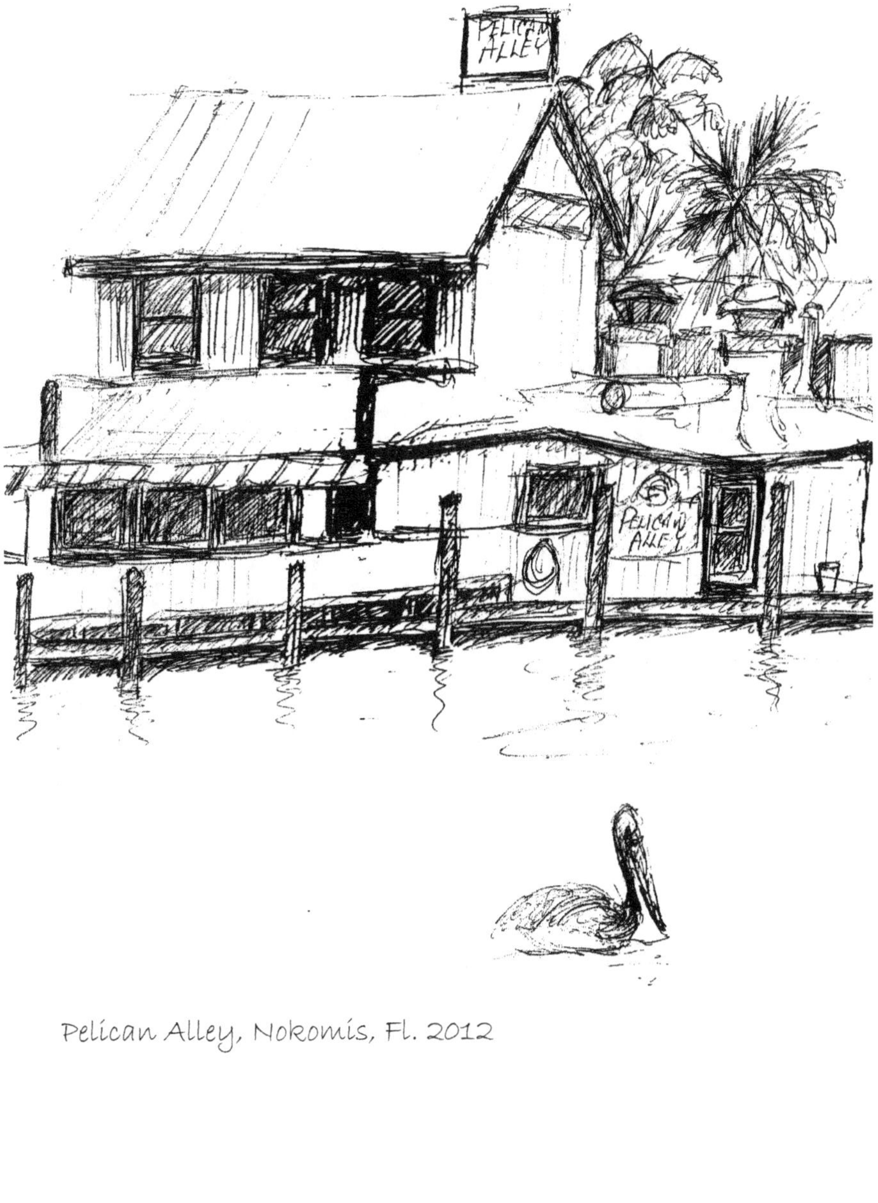

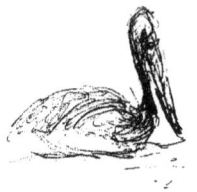

Pelican Alley, Nokomis, Fl. 2012

Feather Marvel

Cross-hatched line
   Interlocking on
Silky-breasted pillow,
Arched wing-flight flappers,
Twitching-tail rudders.
Iridescent oil-slick reds,
   Blues, blacks or
   A clown cacophony.
Bulky puffers and sleek skimmers
Folding upon each other
   For protection.
Tip touches, tickle.
         Nokomis 2015

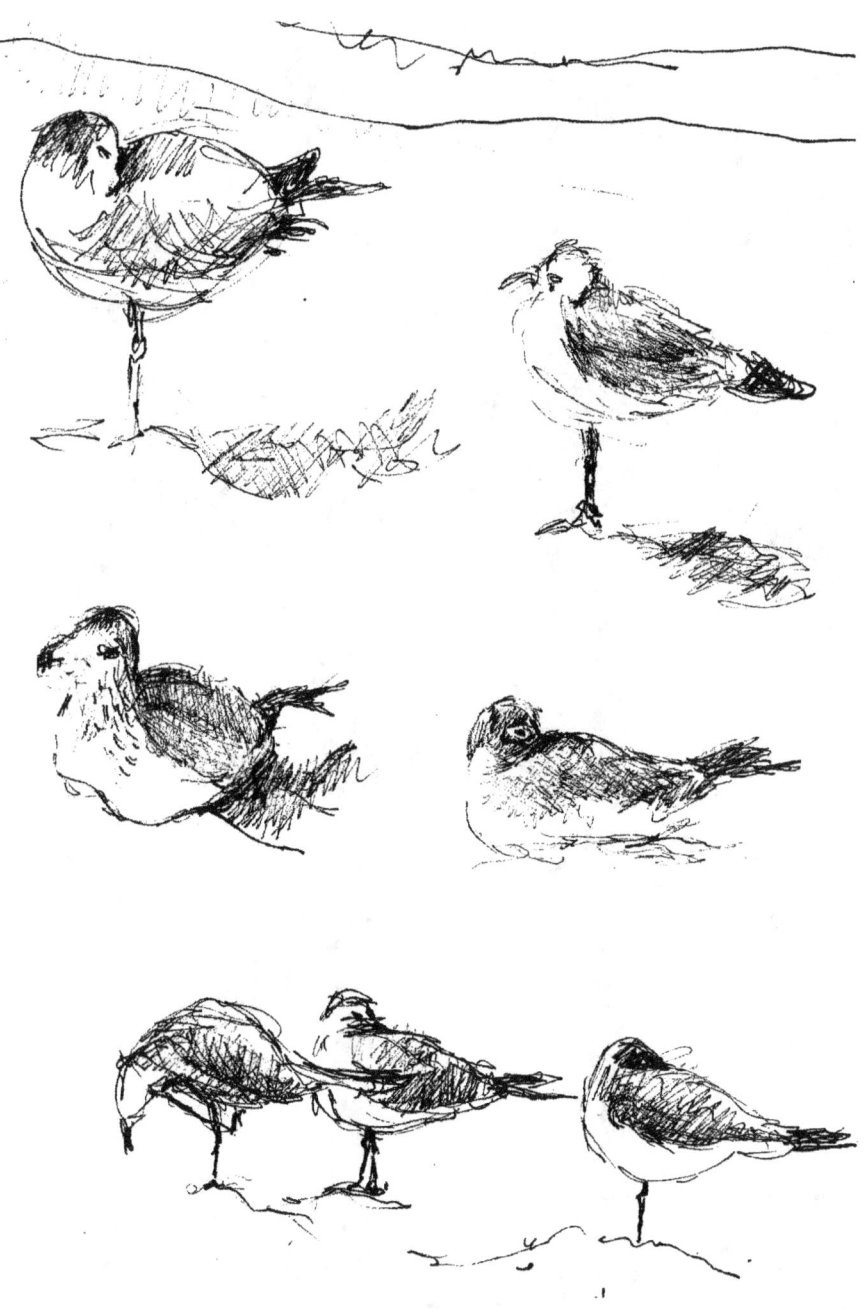

Nokomis Beach, Florida 2014

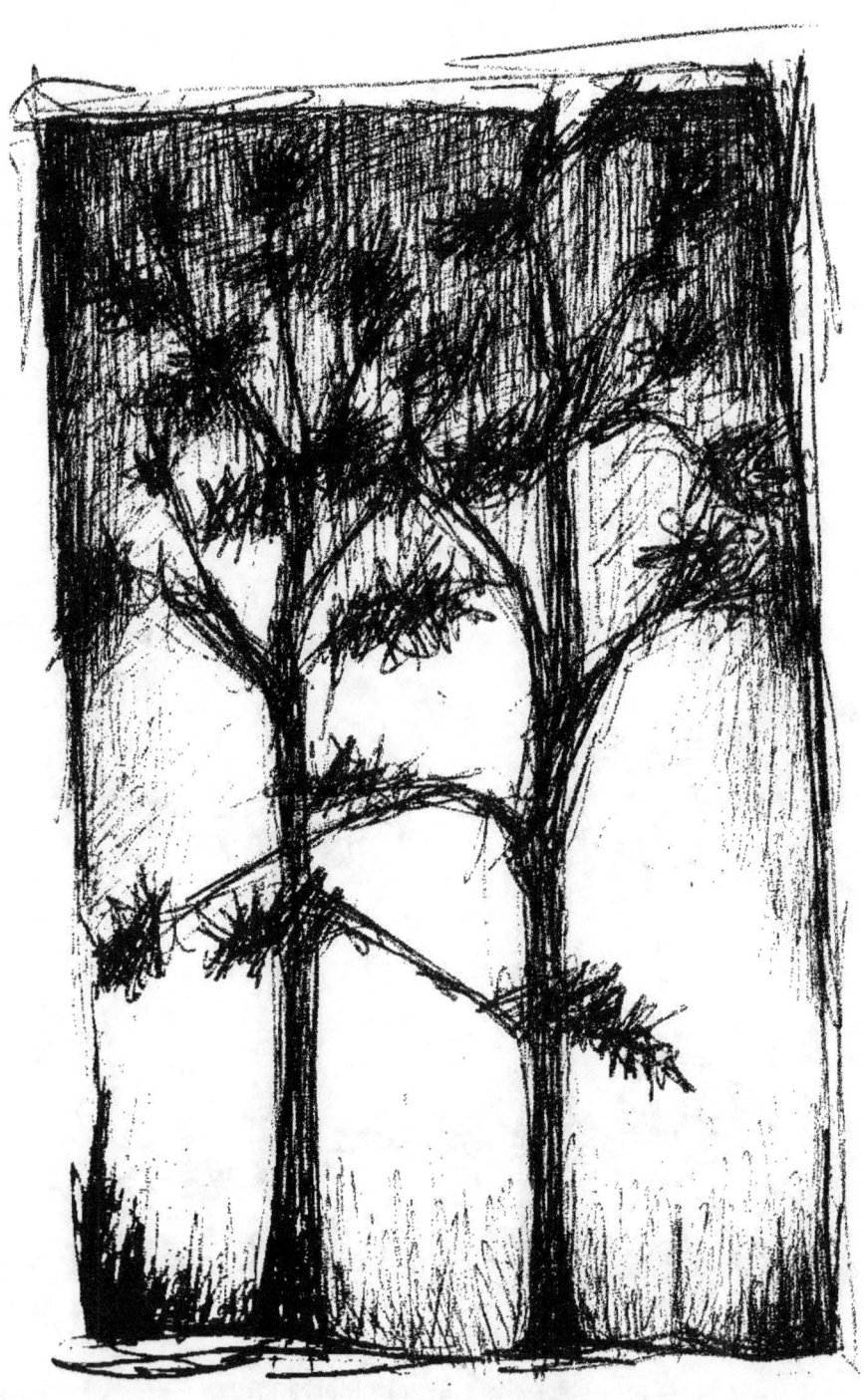

Ft. Meyers, Florida 2015

Looking

Land dichotomy

Loam versus sand

Leaves versus spines

Lowering skies versus shimmering sun

Lazy creeks versus whipped waves

      Lapping at land forms

Lone pines transcend the lapse.

             Nokomis 2013

Stack of Sweaters

I bring my stuff from the north

      That doesn't fit.

The brown painting, the bowl

      Of rocks,

The stacks of sweaters and the

      Drawer of socks.

The memory of chills and

      Grey skies

Are all superfluous in sunshine

      And sandy soil,

But, what if it gets

      Cold and dark?

               Nokomis 2013

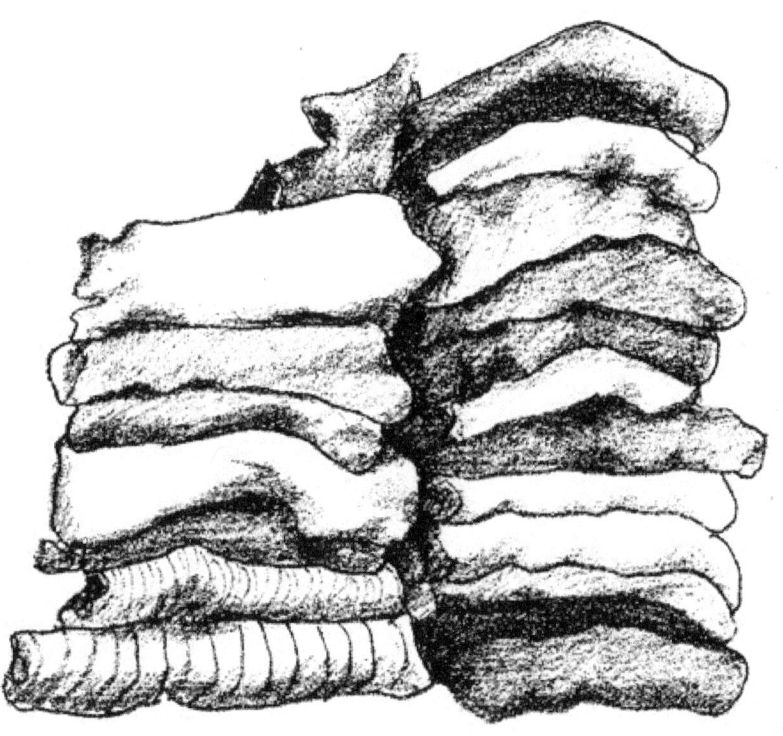

Nokomis, Florida 2013

On Egyptian Art

A magic purpose considered important

With strict adherence to preserving everything.

As a map maker, in perfect clarity

Represents real life drawn in profile

Or its most characteristic angle seen in profile,

Which is strangely flat and contorted.

Not prettiness, but completeness.

Its knowledge of completeness.

Nokomis 2016

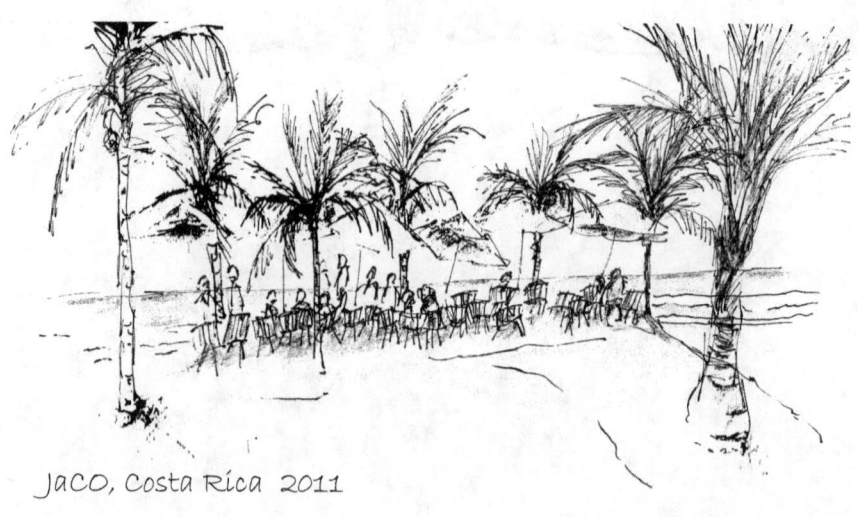

Jaco, Costa Rica 2011

Three Orders

Dominant, Ironic, Corruption.

Sarcastic response to history.

Intellectual, pseudo approach to

Frustration.

It's the crust on a geode.

Nokomis 2016

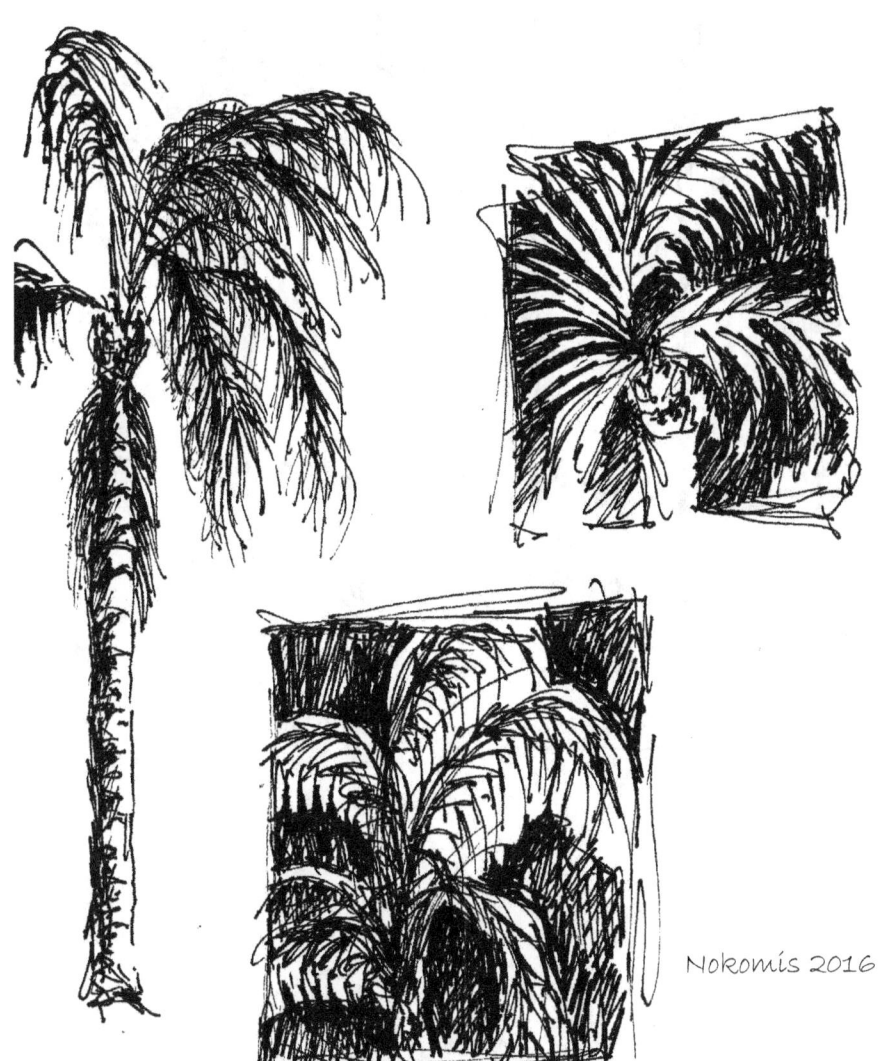

Nokomis 2016

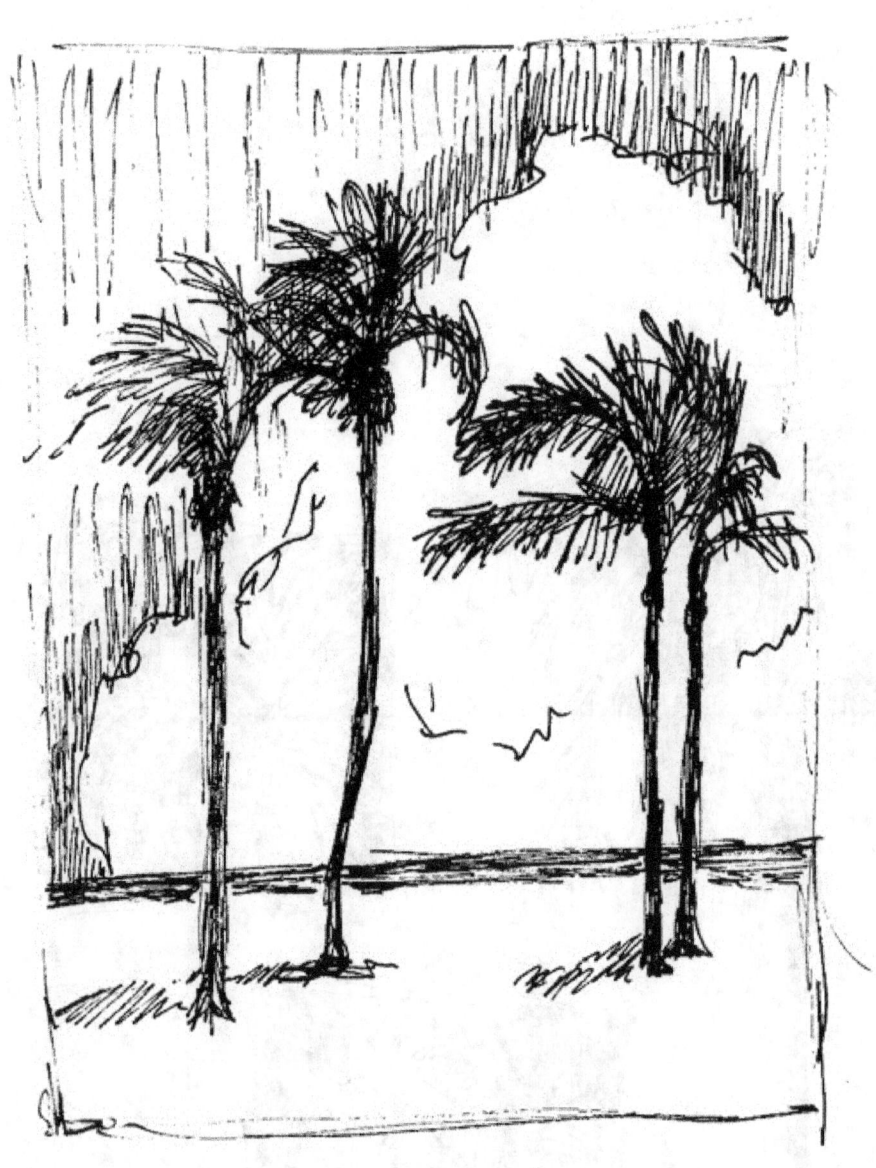

Nokomis 2015

Listen for your Sounds

Even though you are gone
    The sun lights the lake,
    The rain rings on rocks,
    The twilight turns blue.
Even though you are gone
    The robin raises her chicks,
        Outside the shed door,
    The wrens remember their houses
        And sing strident songs,
    The chipmunks check out daily seeds
        Meant for birds.
Even though you are gone
    The laundry spins and bumps,
    The cats pace the floors
        Claiming dog territory.
    The bed holds my bones.
Even though you are gone
    I get up early,
    I moisturize at night,
    I listen for your sounds.
Even though.

              Dewart Lake, Indiana 2007

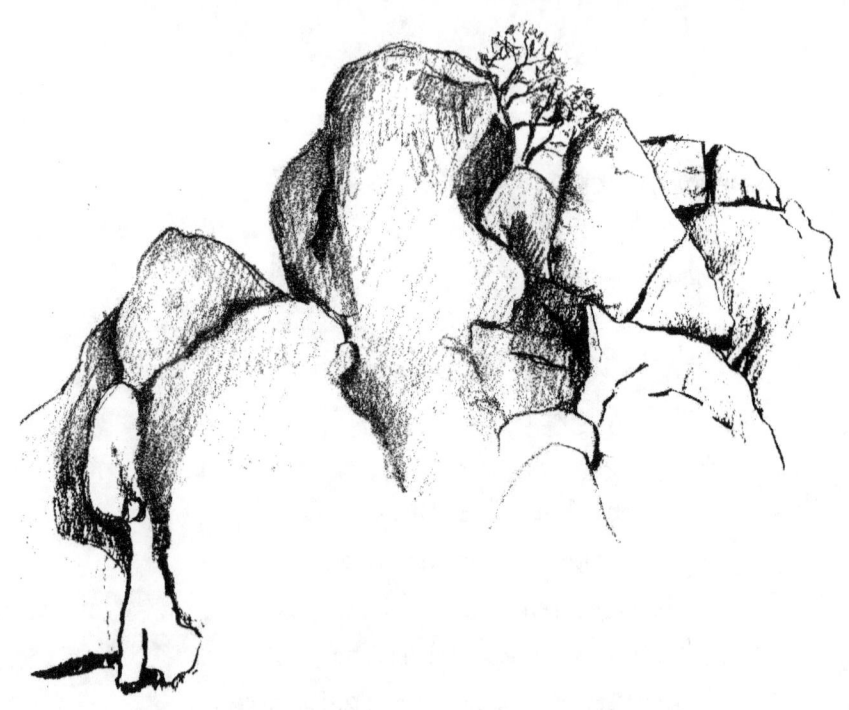

Ruby Mt., Colorado 1998

Boiling Rocks

The buzz is helicopter rides to see
      Lava, flowing orange.
Color power after indigo blue as far as
      The horizon.
They said it boils and blows
      Liquid rock,
New from the earth like
God's hidden hands reaching
      For new life.

Our county has boiling rocks

That show up under the plow

To be seen by man only in spring and fall,

  Old rocks

That have been here before and

  Hidden themselves.

We used to get the old Caravan out,

  Remove the seats, lay down tarp

  And pick those rocks.

We laid them in a patient line

  To guard our drive, outline boundaries,

  Holdup the hill full of flowers.

Now they are sinking

  Like liquid rock

To hide and rise again,

  Boiled like new potatoes.

      Dewart Lake 2007

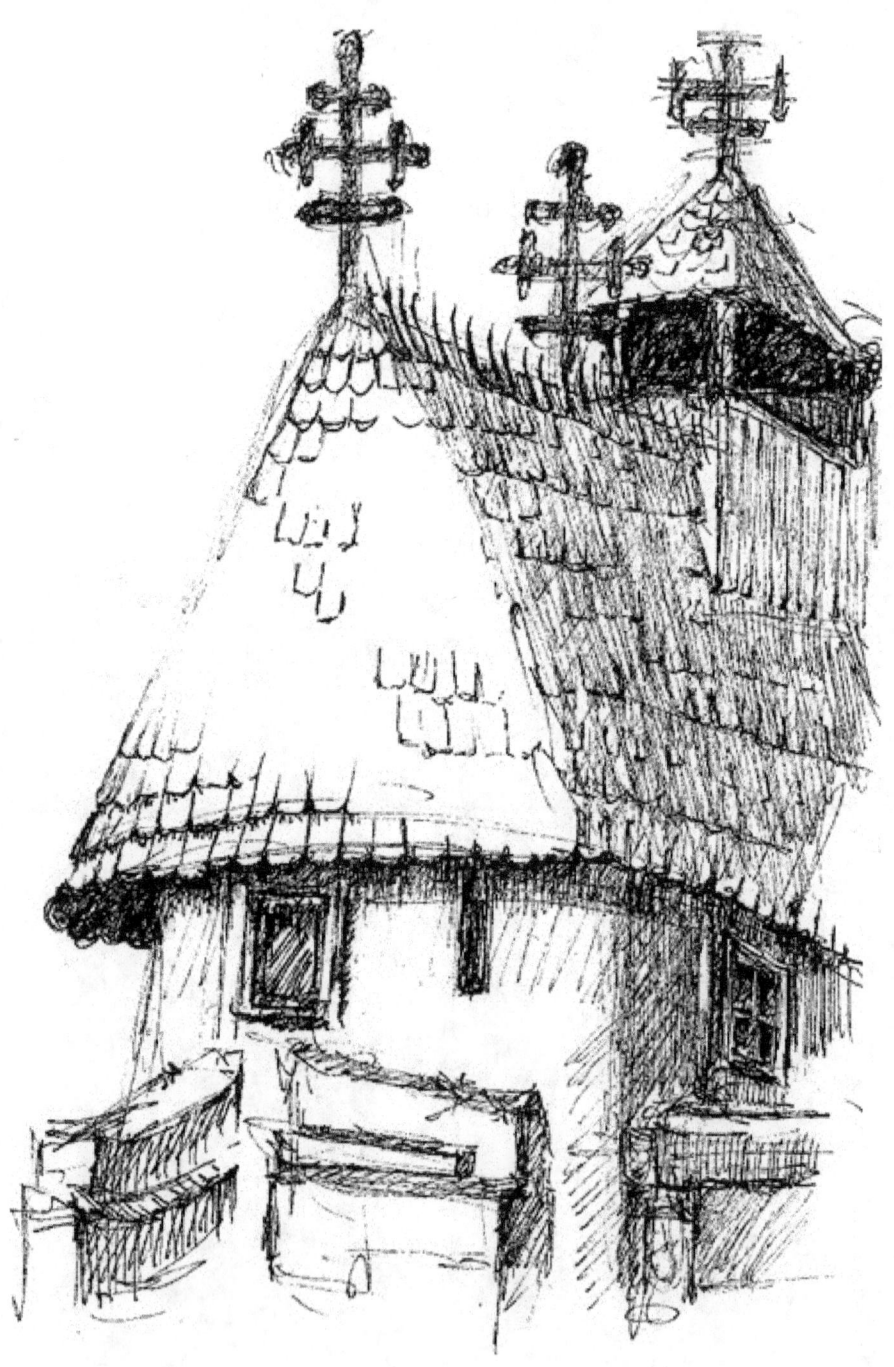

Romania 2015

Grandma

My grandma wore a deep brimmed bonnet
That hung on a backdoor nail in the
      Summer kitchen.
Her rough hen-pecked arms searched gently for
Warm eggs that then nestled in a cotton apron
      Awaiting supper.
She was full of off-key hymns and on-key
      gurgling whistles
As taffy was made from hands full of flour,
      Scoops of sugar and pinches of salt.
A soft pat and low, "Now, Willie..." quieted
      Grandpa Bill's hard of hearing blunders.
Her underwear was chicken skin pink, loose and
      Soft like her downy cheeks.
She smelled faintly of hogs and Teaberry gum
that wafts in my window as I drive on Route 32
      Toward Winchester.
I wanted to be one of those eggs resting in
      An apron
On my grandma's lap.
                Warsaw, Indiana 1999

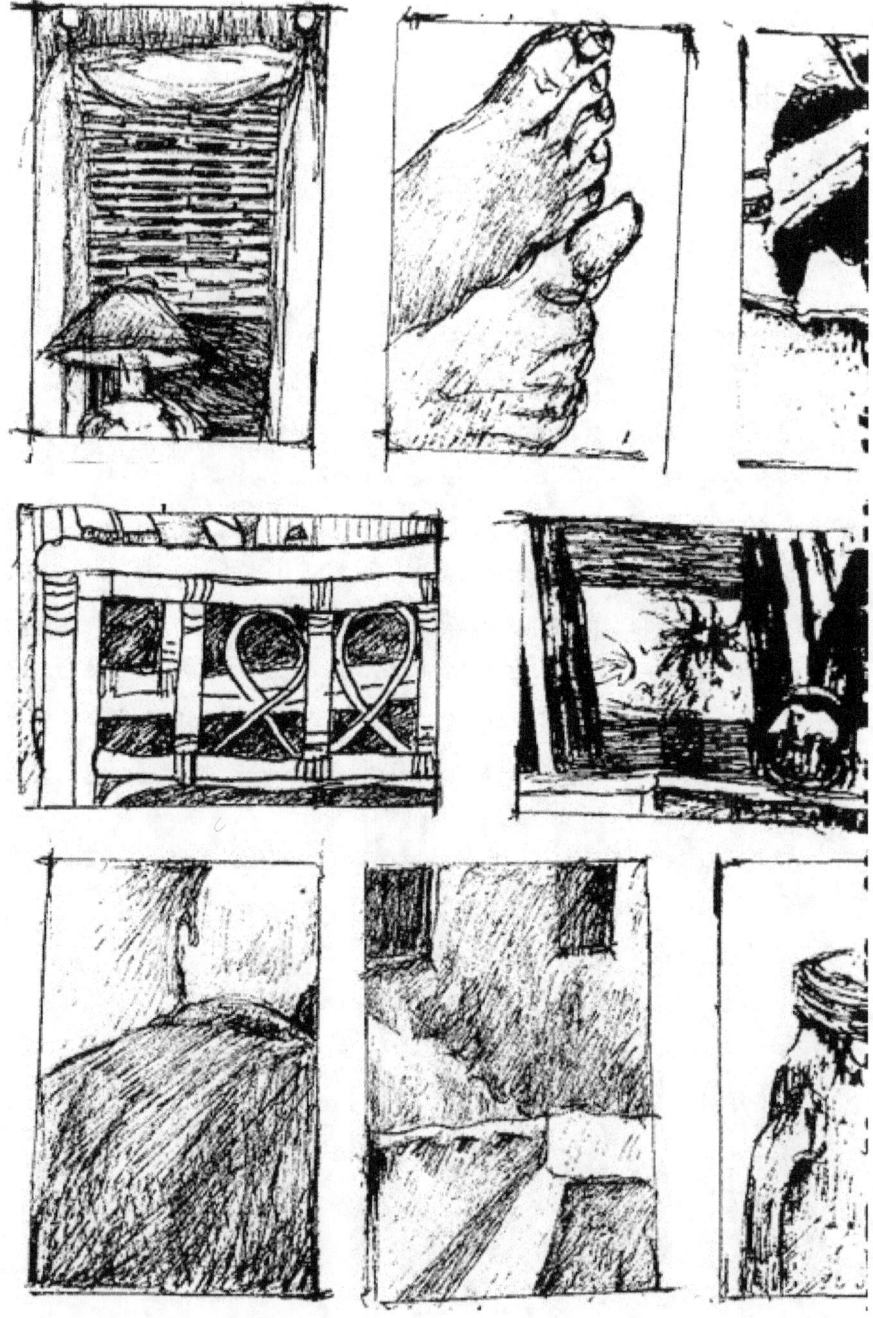

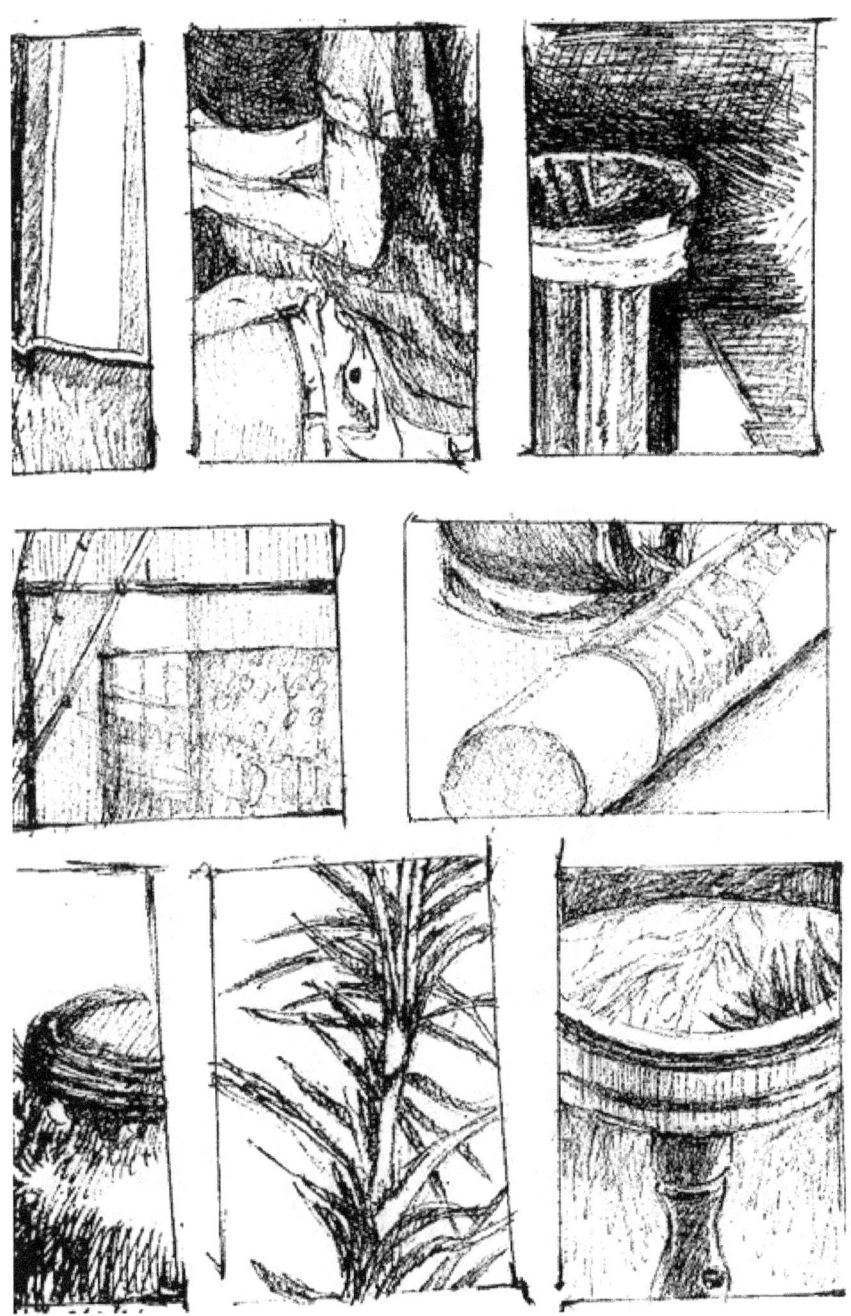

Sketchbook, Nokomis 2014

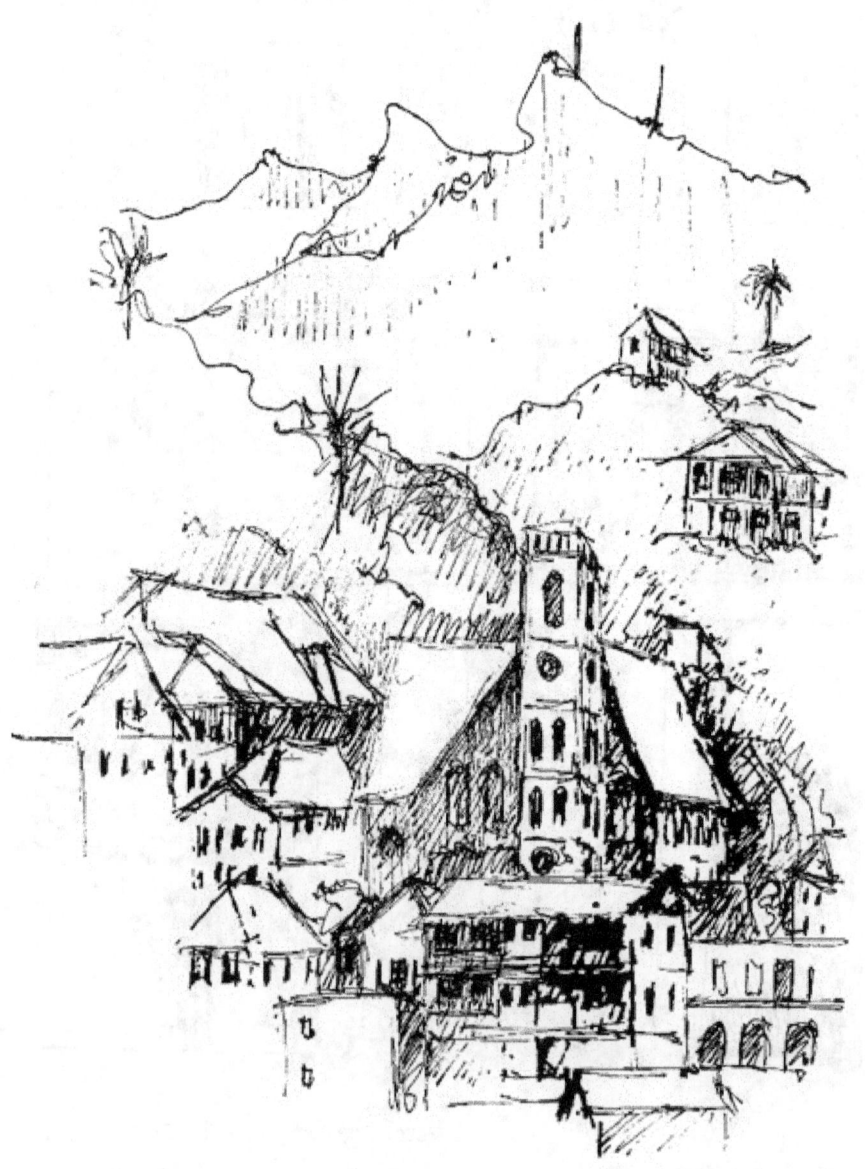

GrENADA 2010

Fall Bullets

Soybeans are turning yellow,

Cicadas are quieting their din,

Corn is drying up,

Wooley worms are crossing the road,

Bark stopped splitting off the sycamores,

Morning is a little chilly,

Robins are gone,

Spiders are webbing big,

Birds are returning to the feeders,

I'm closer to dying.

Syracuse, Indiana 2007

Chair

Child's chair

      In a kindergarten classroom,

Discarded, disregarded, yet tough

      Abandoned for steel.

Once red, then brown,

      Played on, sat on, stood on.

Now prized for a memory marker

      And it endures.

              2016, Nokomis

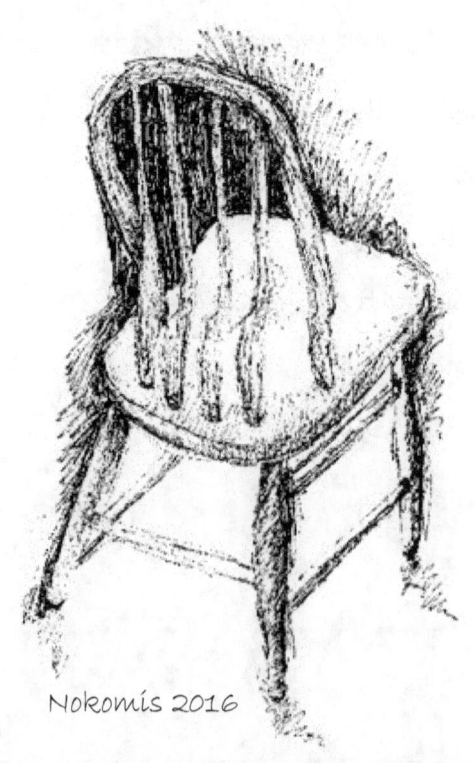

Nokomis 2016

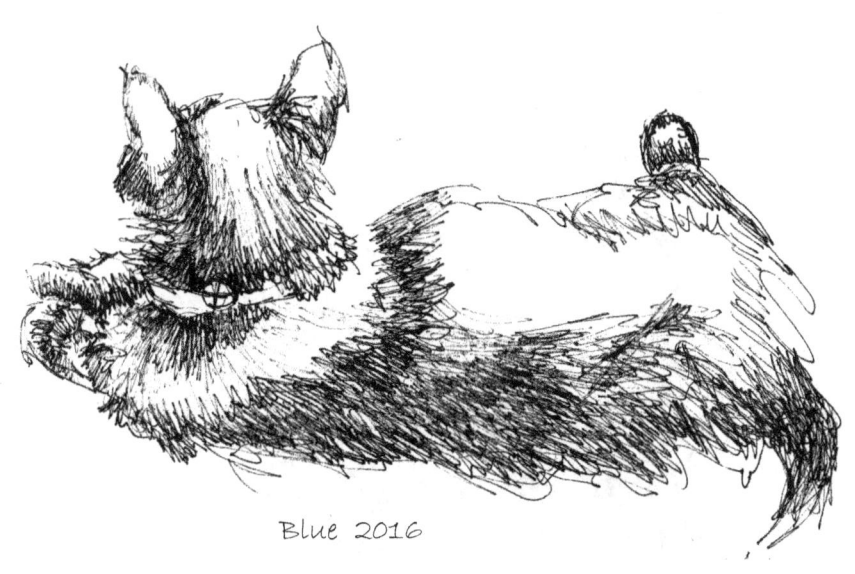

Blue 2016

Blue Cat

Sun spotter, soft sleeper,

Bowl checker, crunch eater,

Leg licker, paw patter,

Bug catcher, bird watcher,

Rug rubber, butt bather,

Human handler, meow murmur.

It's all about absorption.

2016, Nokomis

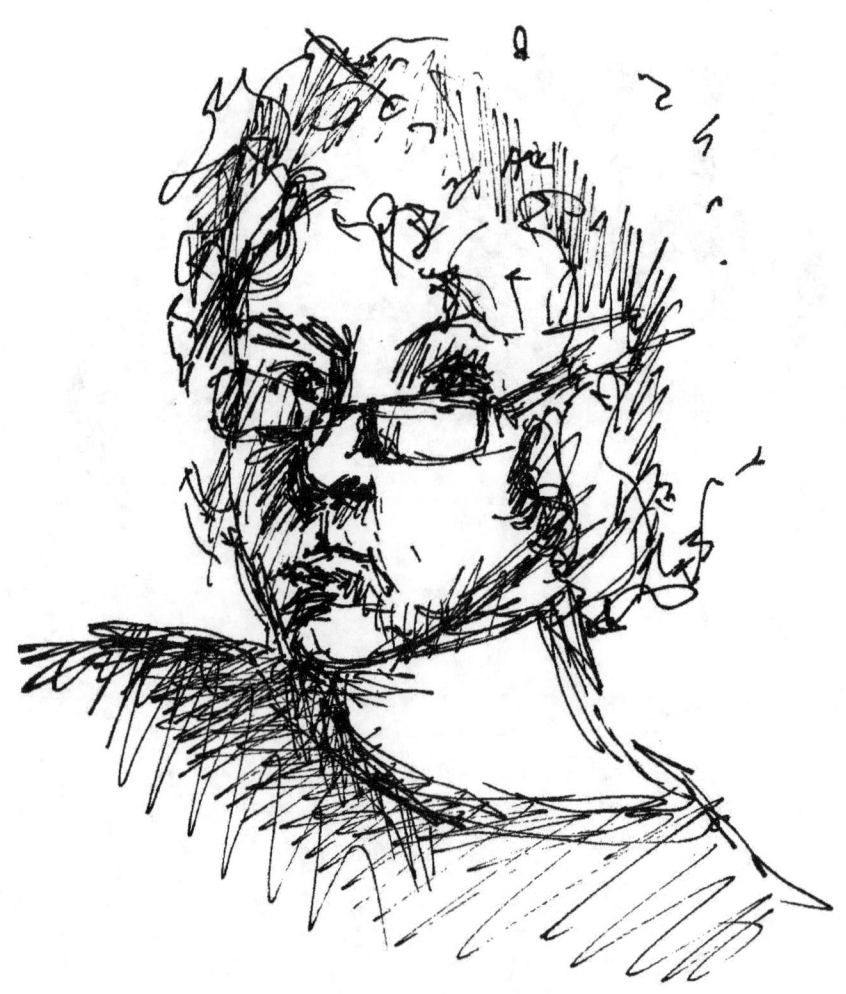

Italy 2014

Mom

She shakes her head

Confirmation

Ready

After bra, panties, hose, garter belt, slip, dress, belt,

    Jewelry, makeup, comb, lipstick,

    Lower lip first.

I arose this morning,

    Fed cats, peed, weighed, washed, combed,

makeup,

    Mirrored my face.

I shook my head in surprise.

Syracuse, Indiana 2008

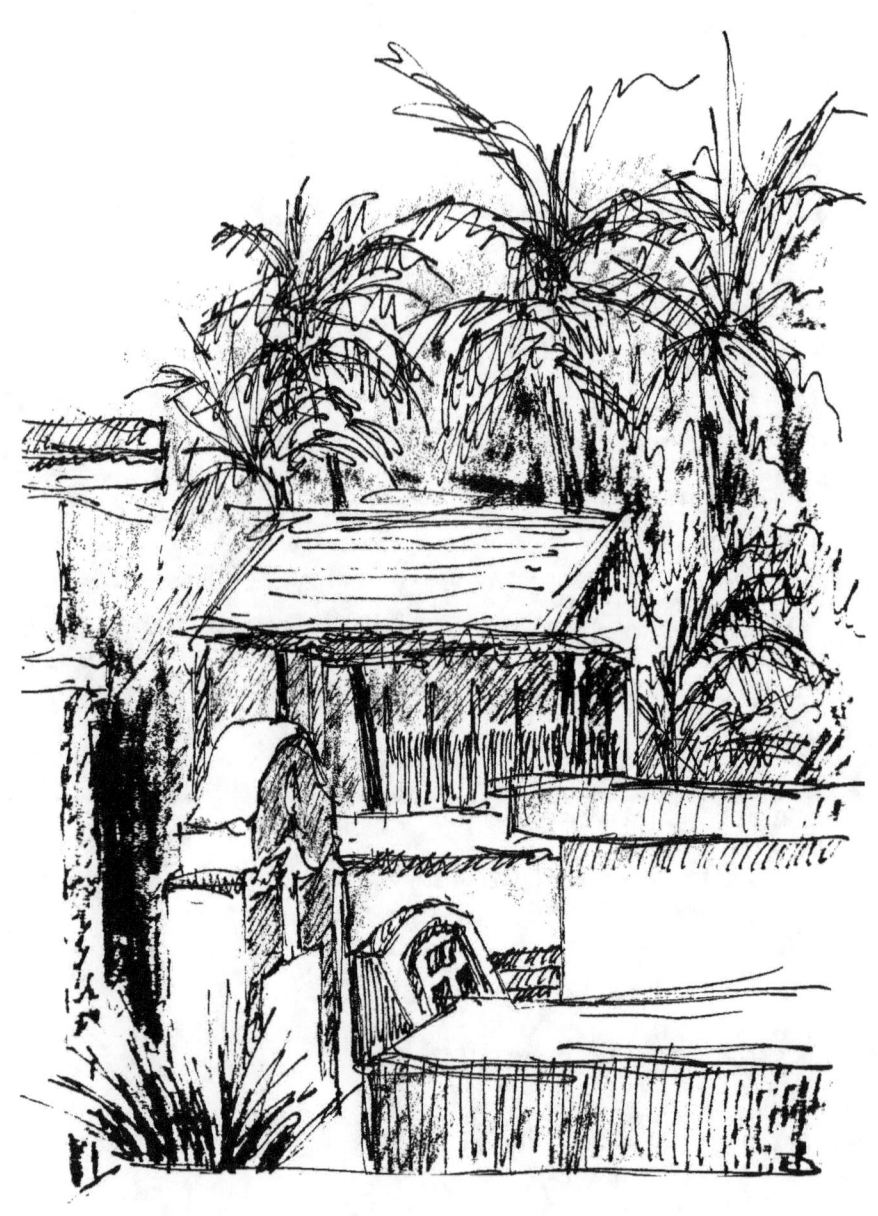

Key West, Florida 2013

Lullaby Lacking

The sea rocks a gentle lullaby

      While the azure hues calm the eyes.

The babble of staccato cadence form a murmur

      Of inane immediacy.

There are times to talk and not talk,

But all forget the value of silence so God

      Has room to dwell.

Sorry God, no room for you and your

      Sweet sayings.

My ears are full.

               Nokomis, Florida 2015

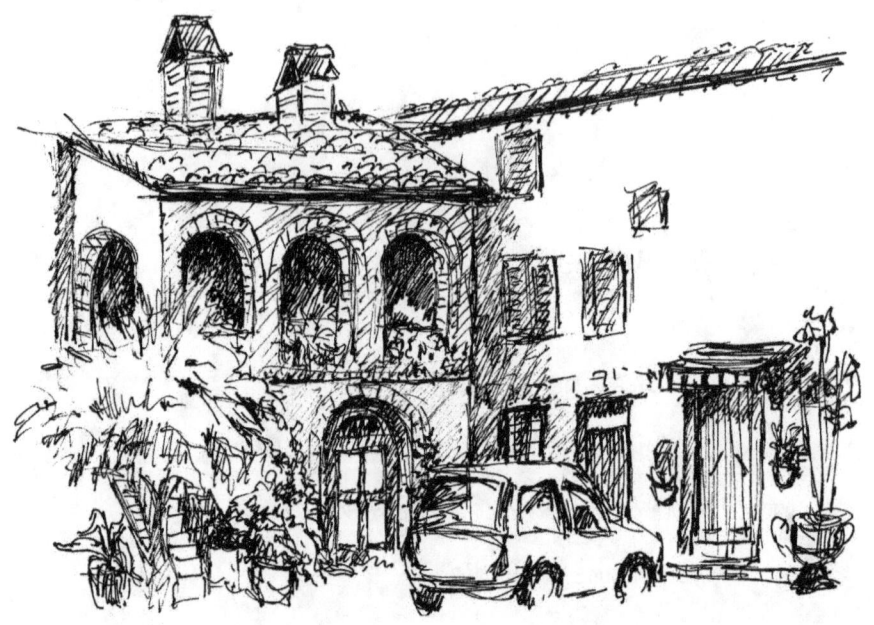

Italy 2014

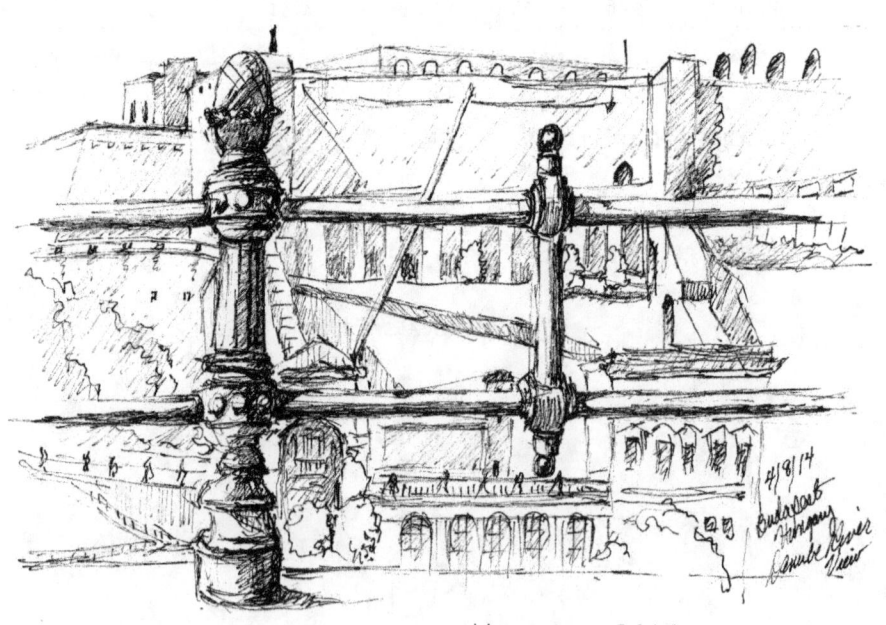

Hungary 2014

Grandpa Bill

Grandpa Bill, as an old farm man

      Announced at dinner's end

      In his Bartonie brogue,

"Ya know, if you was a dyin'

      And et a pickle, I believe

      Yad jis go on ahead and die!"

I laughed, but a pickle isn't a meal.

      It's salty, dill, bitey, savory,

      Sometimes teeth-achingly sweet.

      It's an accent.

When I was sixteen, I snagged my first

      Store-bought fancy coat.

Black, fake-furry, soft, iridescent,

      Night dark, cowl-collared and

      Oh, so elegant.

Not hand-me-down Betty's, nor hand-made sewn,

      It was a pickle!

              Nokomis 2016

Shooting Star

I'm missing voids; solitude,

      Darkness, quiet.

As an eight year old, I saw the

      Milky Way streaming across the

      Dark sky.

I've seen it once more in middle age, out west,

      While listening to a fish jump and a cricket

      Rudely rub its legs.

The sky sent a shooting star and

      I swear I could hear it,

      It was soft silent.

Now that I am old, even time

      Leaks away, so quickly, so easily.

I lie in bed, waiting for the traffic gap,

      So I can gather singular silence.

                        Nokomis, Florida 2016

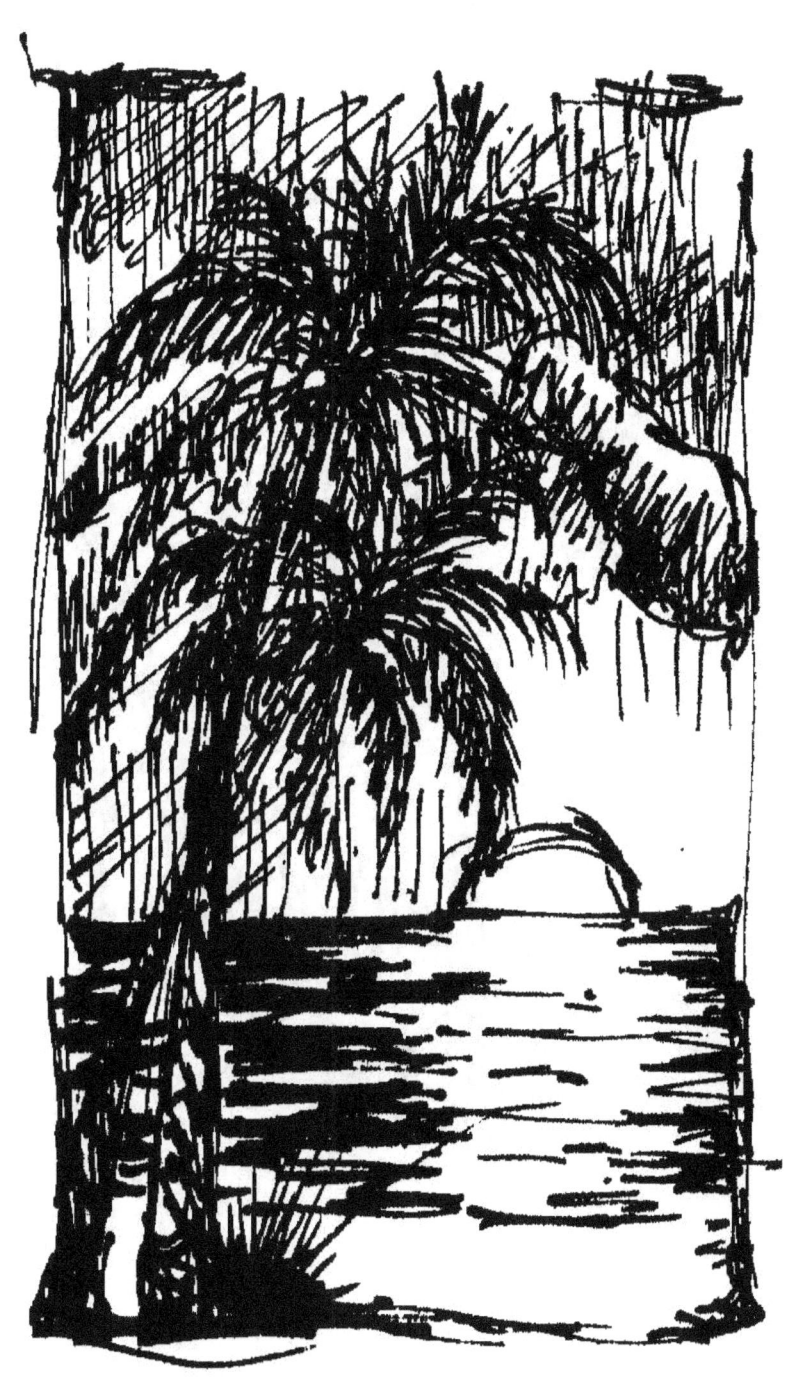

Nokomis, Florida 2016

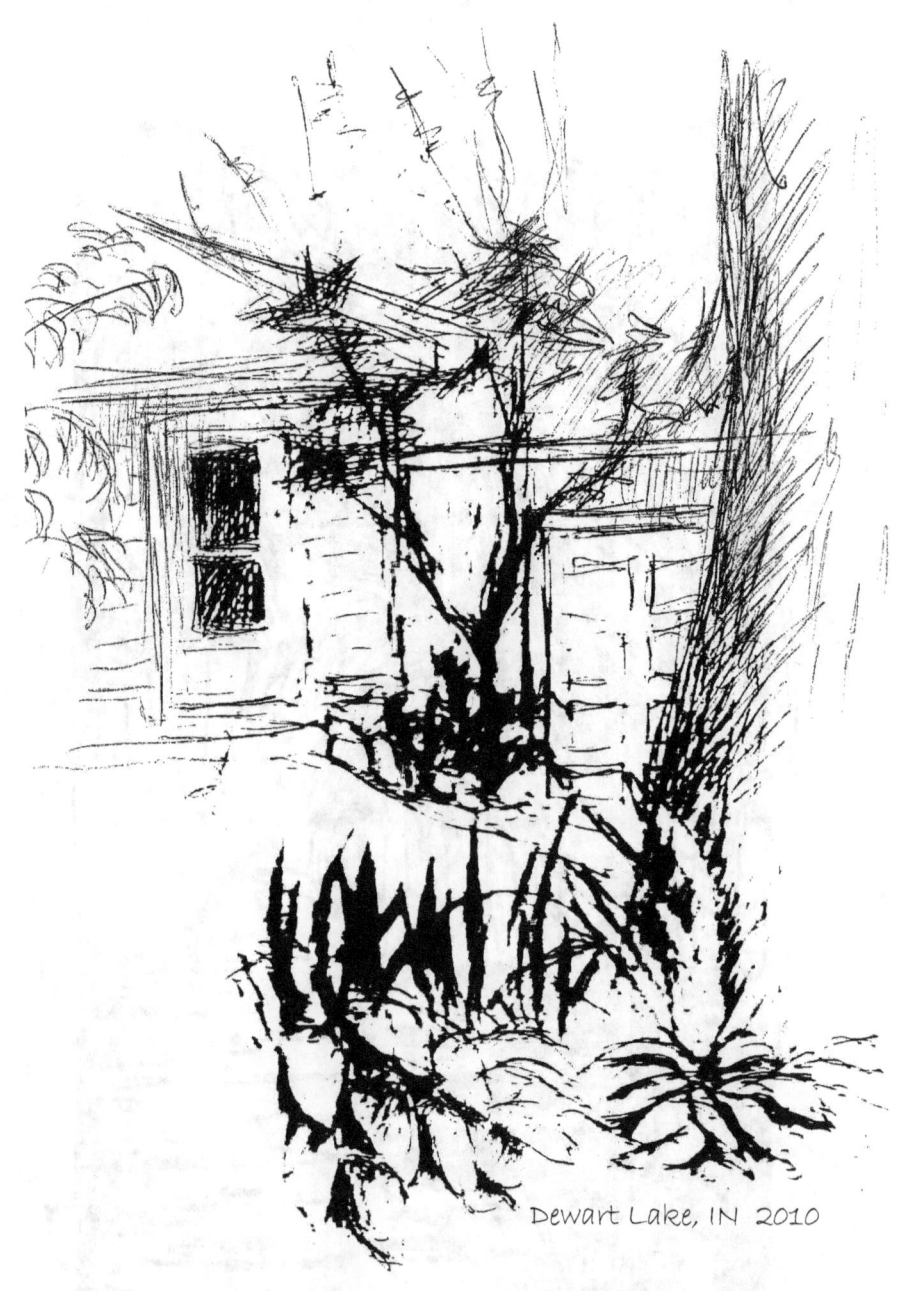

Dewart Lake, IN 2010

Sleep Music

Encased in rubber, a wire rests against a familiar tree.

    It groans and scratches each movement.

The tree is sturdy, I cannot see its trunk move,

    But the scritch-scratch tells the tale

    Like raucous music.

In the beginning it annoyed, like bold ice cubes dumping

    Into their tray,

But now, years later, it's a lullaby

    Recording the wind.

                    Dewart Lake, Indiana 2008

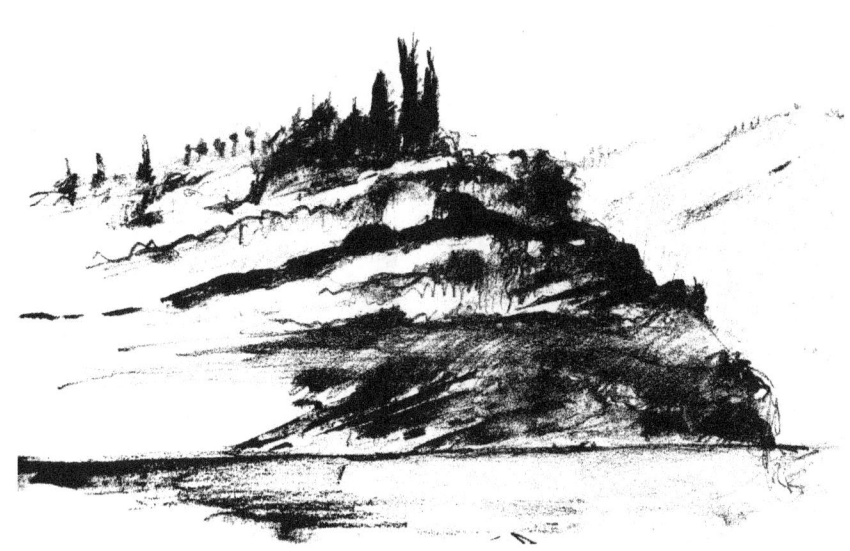

Yangtze River, China 2001

Too Many Goodbyes

You left, she left, he left

     They moved.

At the airport, left my bag in the car,

     Another goodbye.

Goodbye means God be with you,

     God be with me.

Tim said, "We grew apart, found our own ways."

     Another goodbye.

Celebration flowers in red, yellow, white, pink

     Mark the past years.

Wilted trash, goodbye.

Cleaning closets,

     Al's lidded pot, Old cream jar, Dad's

prized pear print,

     Chase's cherry table, Mom's tomato

masher,

     Grandma's platform rocker?

     Goodbye.

No, please, not yet.

                    Syracuse, 2007

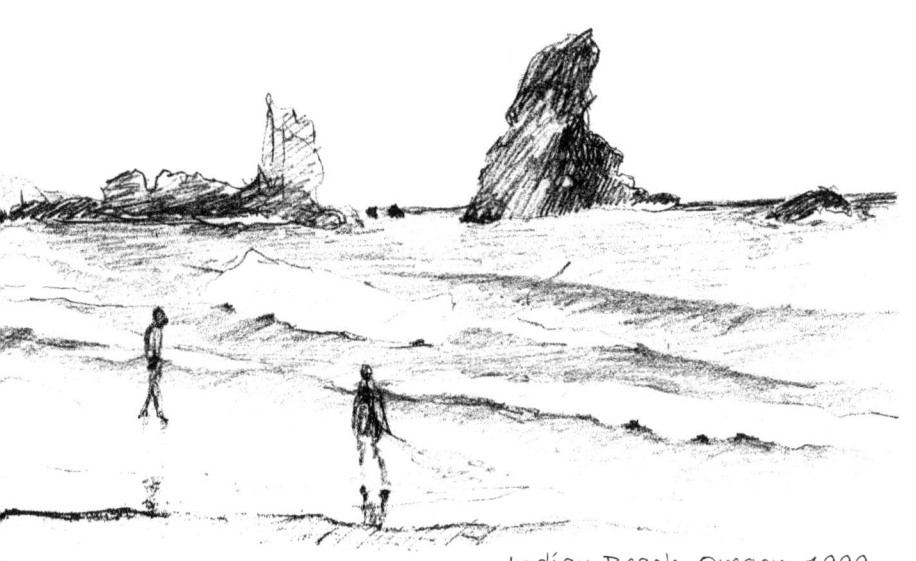

Indian Beach, Oregon 1999

Secret Life of Birds

The river gently drifts its way

     To the bay

Carrying leaf bits while shielding the

     Brown debris under the surface.

Traffic continues its frantic pace

     To condos, stores, dealers,

But the quiet breeze ripples the leaves of water

     While bugs search for fish.

The sound of a lone bird marking territory

     Interrupts a secret splash,

The silent swoop of a purposeful

     Great blue heron

Startles my mute drawing and I

     Forget what I was doing.

(Whilst sitting at the boat launch on Salt Creek.)

     Nokomis, Florida 2016

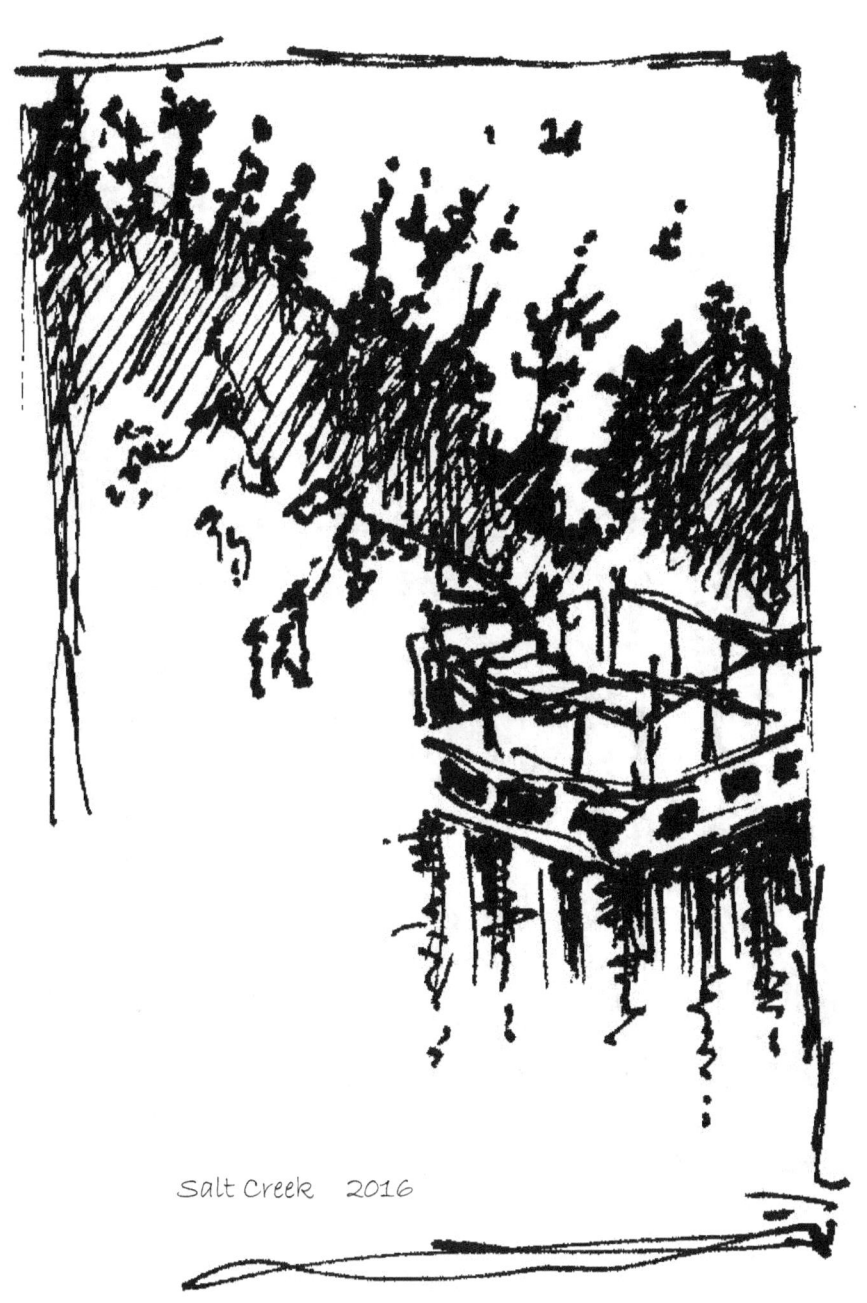

Salt Creek   2016

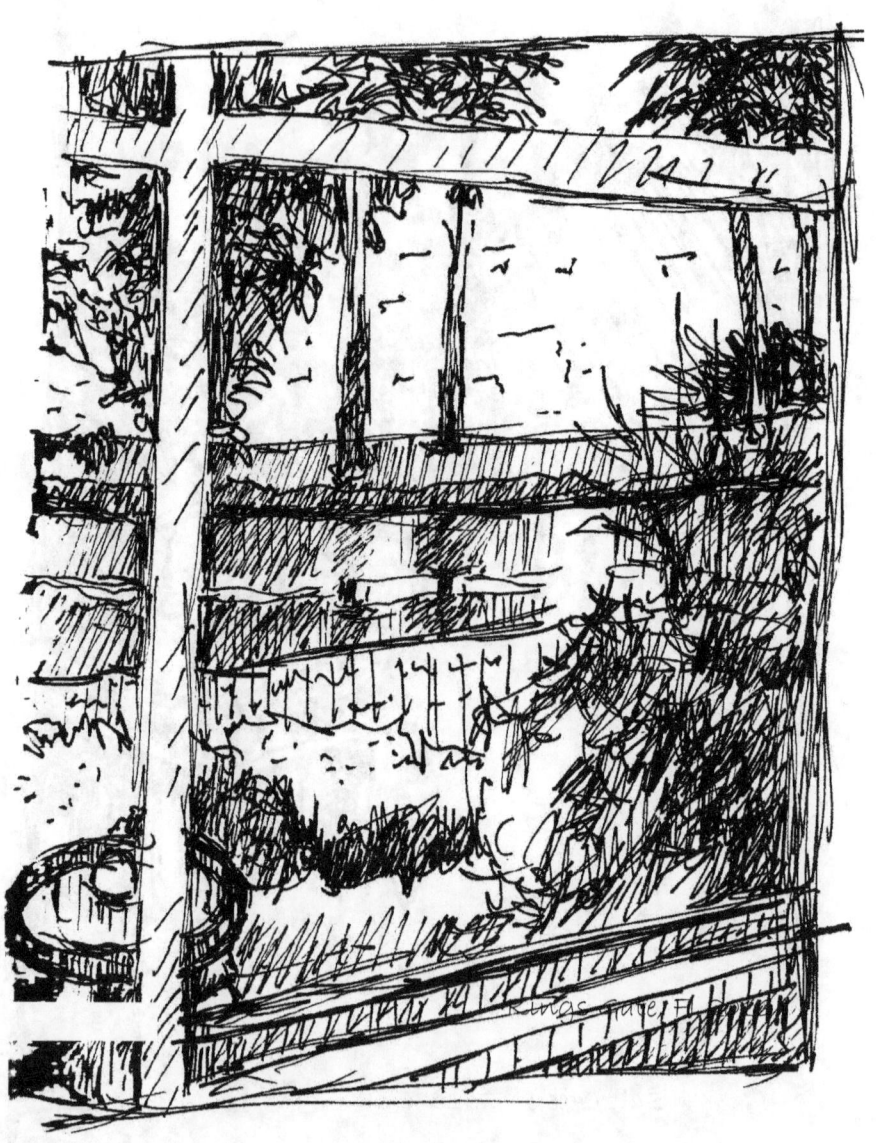

King's Gate, Florida, 2015

Paper Hands

My grandmother had small paper hands
      But they could work.
When I knew her, they folded in her lap
      As she rocked in an armless black patterned
      Rocker.
Her hand covered her mouth when she laughed
      And aunts and uncles laughed when she did.
She was the cue.
We ate on rainbow dishes,
      But I never saw her wash one.
In fourth grade, I was a giant to her,
      But her son was a giant to me.
Her hands dusted many pitchers
      Brought to her by loving sons and daughters.
She was a grocery woman.
My dad cried when she died
      With his hand over his mouth.

                1990, about Ida Opal Hoback Stoops
                Warsaw, Indiana

Touching Stones

Reading a book by gloves and hat,

    As I read by sunlight and heat.

Eating rice and beans,

    As I eat eggs and bacon and toast.

Walking uphill on cobblestones,

    As I walk on figured carpet.

Sleeping under layered blankets,

    As I sleep under comforter bagged.

Talking in mysterious sounds,

    As I talk in inanities.

Words are the stones that cast rings of connection,

    Pauses for time and understanding.

Letters that say little, but mean so much,

    Spaces that stutter questions and wondering.

Fabric pulled taut, threads straining for connection,

    Warp is strong, the weft is weak.

Mother's connection, one so intense,

    Now she lets go, she lets me go.

You become the stone she touches,

    As do I.

Syracuse, Indiana 2007

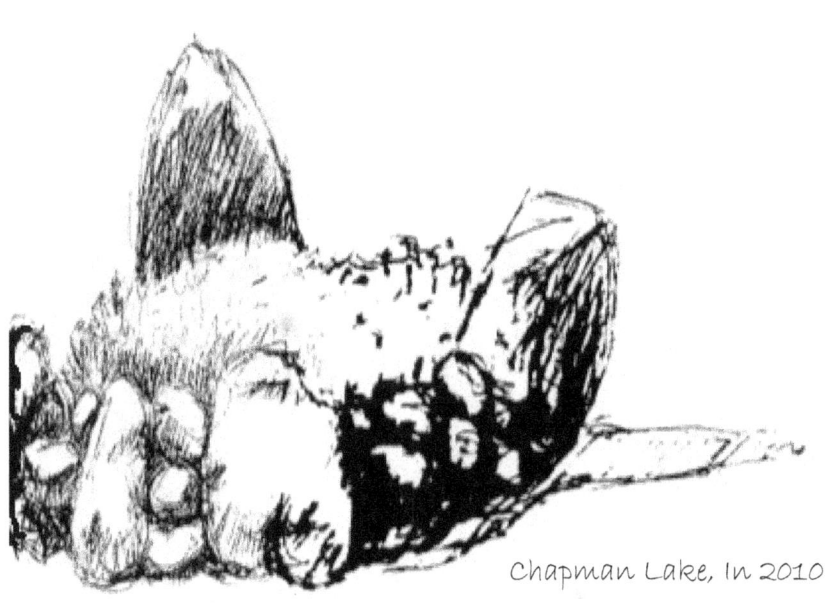

Chapman Lake, In 2010

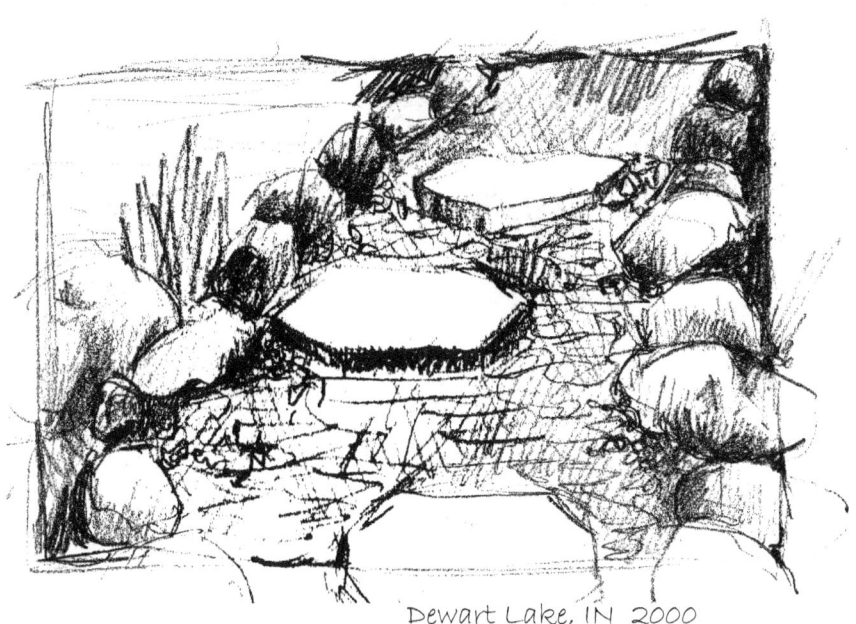

Dewart Lake, IN 2000

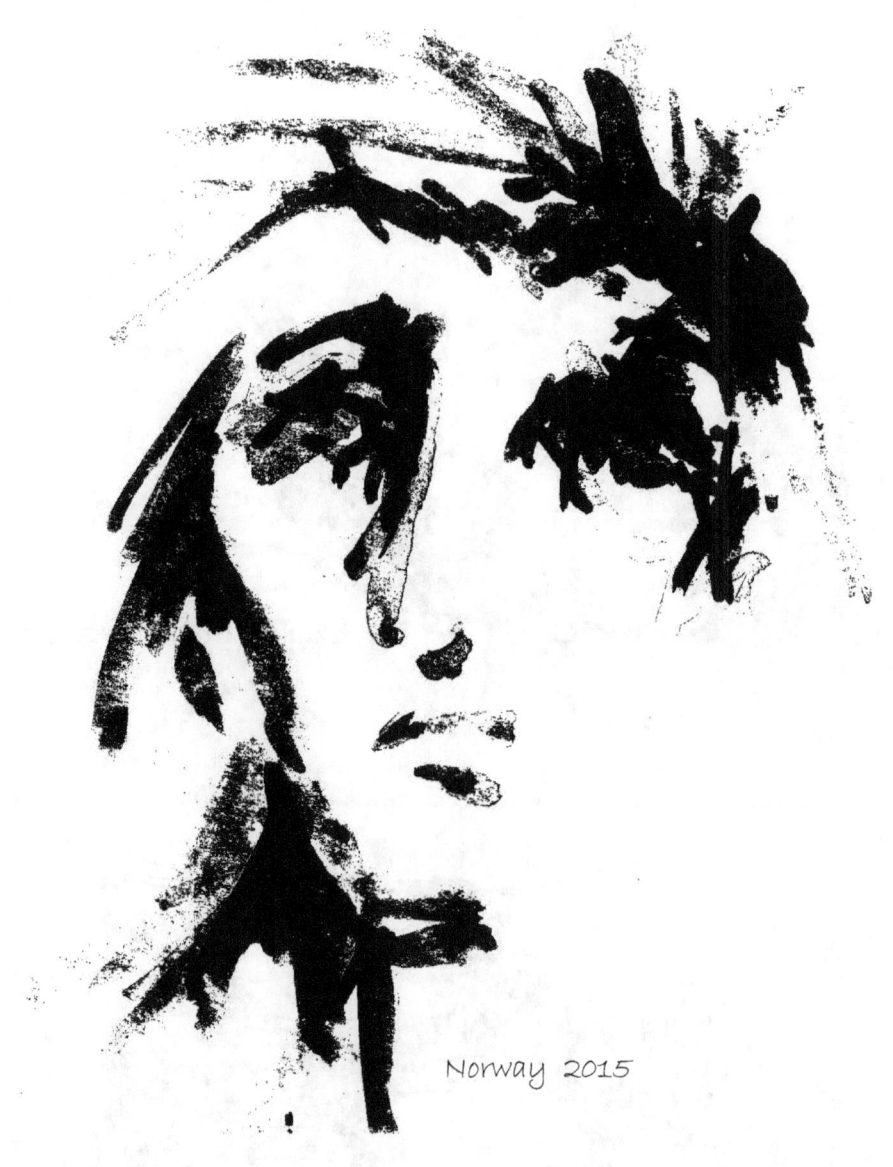

Norway 2015

TV

I like TV.

It passes the time

When I get bored

With my life.

Nokomis, Florida 2013

You Gone

My steps ascend
Quiet padded soles
Celestial morning glow
Movement begins
With flutters
I turn and find
You gone
As I lie in bed.

Dewart Lake   2008

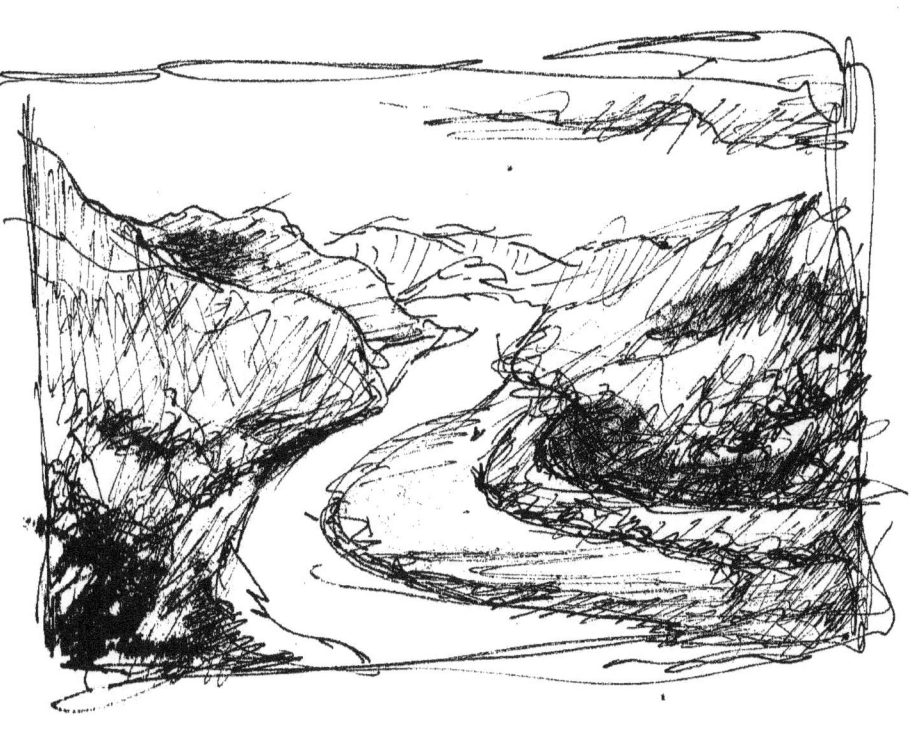

Out West   2014

Upper Room

Went to Grandma Bill's when I was 12.

Slept in Mom and Dad's lofty room

Facing the long fields of corn.

A big round mirrored make-up table sat

      Low and wide with linen doilies and drawers.

Rippled green and transparent

      Comb, brush and mirror on one side,

China cats played on the other.

      Different poses, I rearranged each day.

Alone in that sunset room, I waited

      With empty longing.

The train complaining of loneliness

      At forty acres distance

I hear it call,

      Even today.

                Syracuse, Indiana   2008

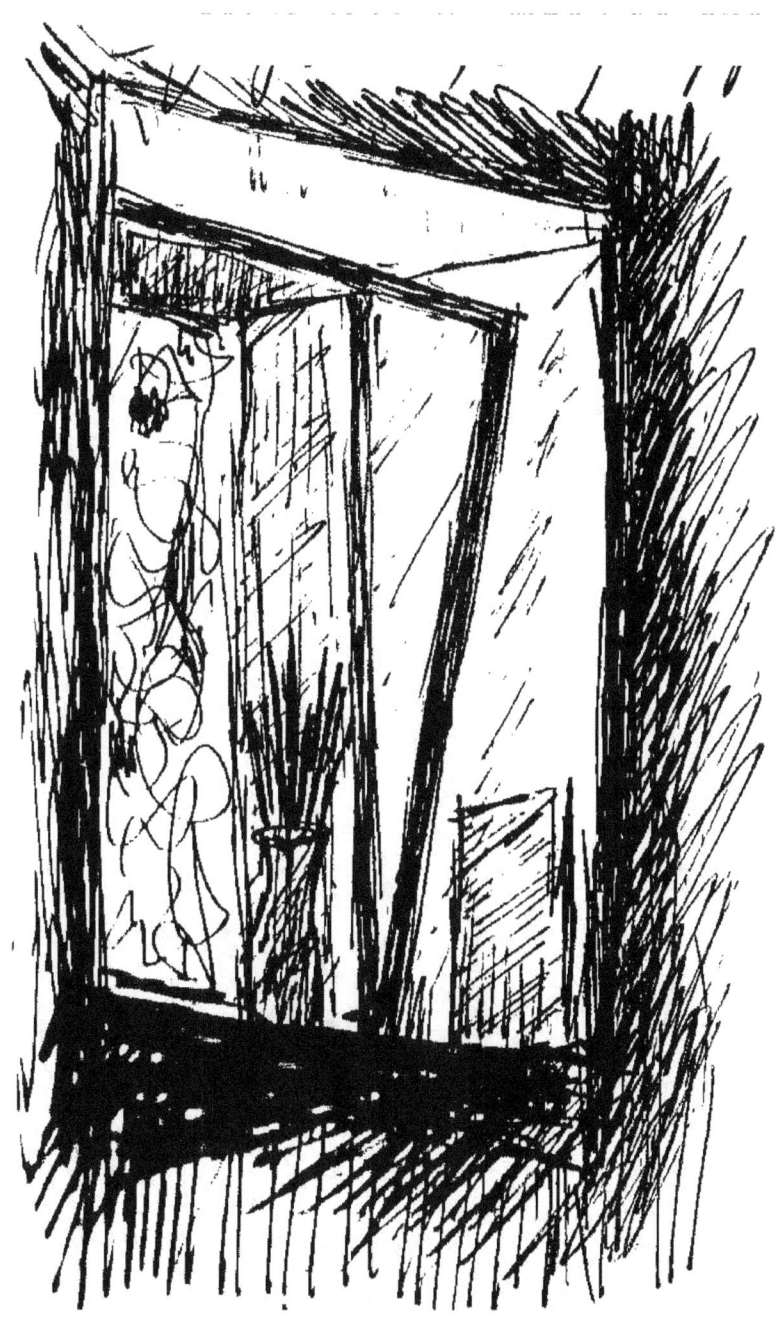

Will's Window
Farnese, Italy 2014

The Wall

The wall wraps me, an illusion of snug safety

      Eliminating space, speed and sound.

The wall deflects detail, directs focus

      Upward to cloud sky scene.

The wall frames plants, transforming into

      Shadow sketches, a silhouette style.

The wall traps trees and prevents

      Plodding palms from marching away.

The wall woos the scorning sneer

      Of birds.

                Kings Gate 2016

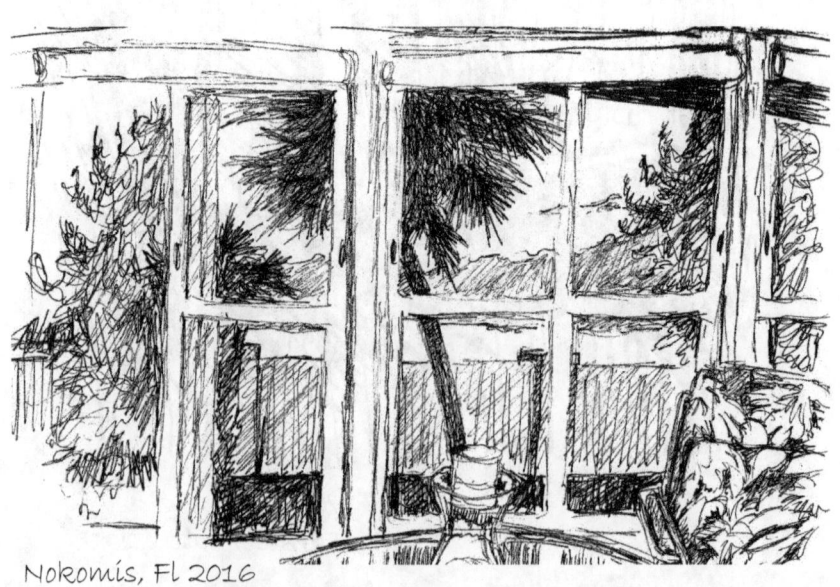

Nokomis, Fl 2016

This House

This metal house beats its drum head under sheets of rain
> To become rivers that shift sand to the sea.
> Woodpecker attacks compete with raw rhythm.

How ironic that this lake paradise is desert sand where
> Cactus nestles happily against banana leaves and
> bougainvillea.

Reptiles and rabbits feed side by side waiting patiently for
> Predator picks.
> Only the bobcats and alligators prevail.

This Florida house sits uneasily on tropical shifting sand
> Perched ready to be blown up into mountain clouds
> That billow with luxurious warmth and mist.

The sun seeks its metal cracks to snake in, robbing the cool
> Refrigerated of its comfort.

Wave after wave of noisy vehicles trek by its doors
> Seeking silence of roaring waters.

Sanctuary of this house is contained by a white wall
> That's cracked.

Nokomis, Florida 2014

Silence

It explodes, huge sounds round and

Empty.

Who said it's golden?

Its fullness opens my senses

Instead of blankets of distractions.

Cats padding, rain on rock, train's dying whistle

Silence is alone,

Healing me with quiet.

Dewart Lake, Indiana 2007

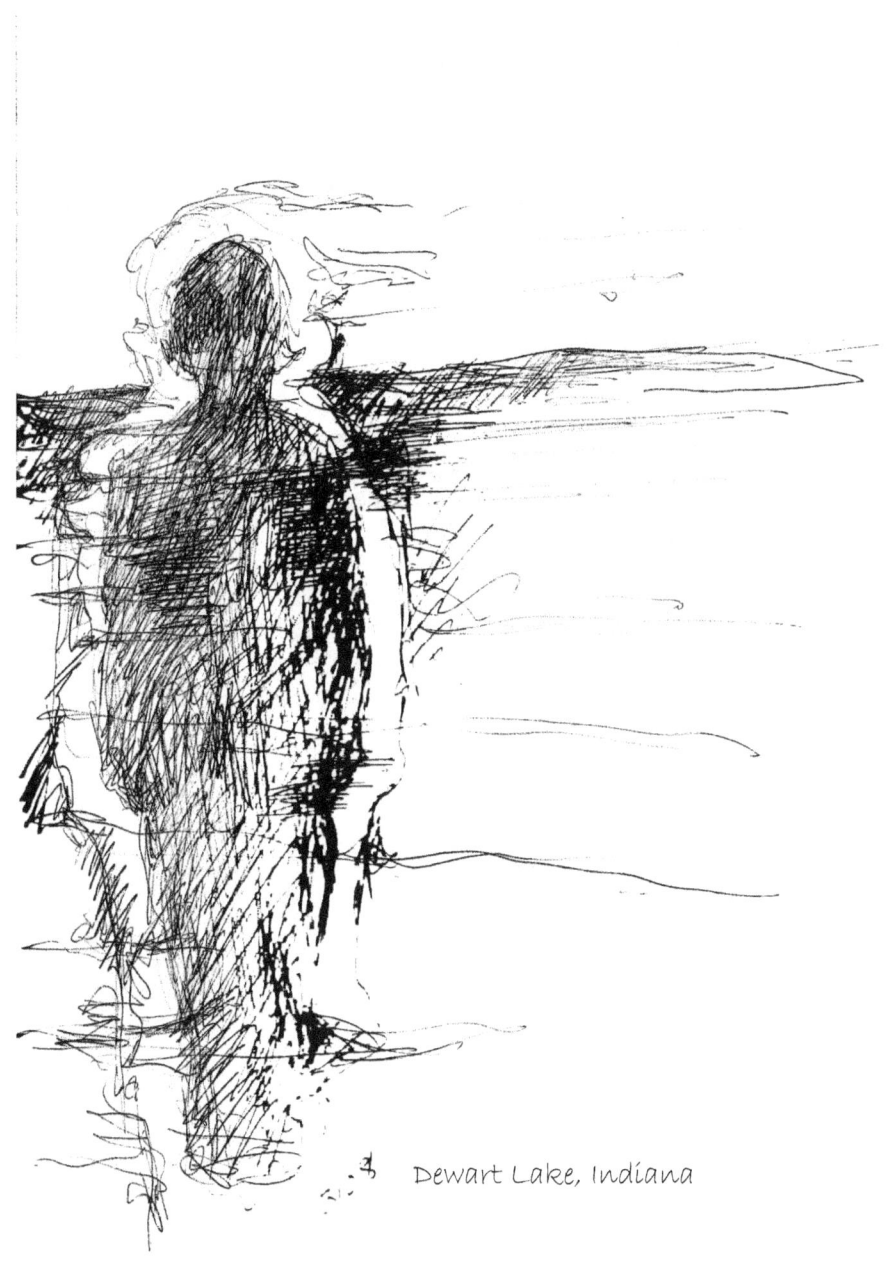

Dewart Lake, Indiana

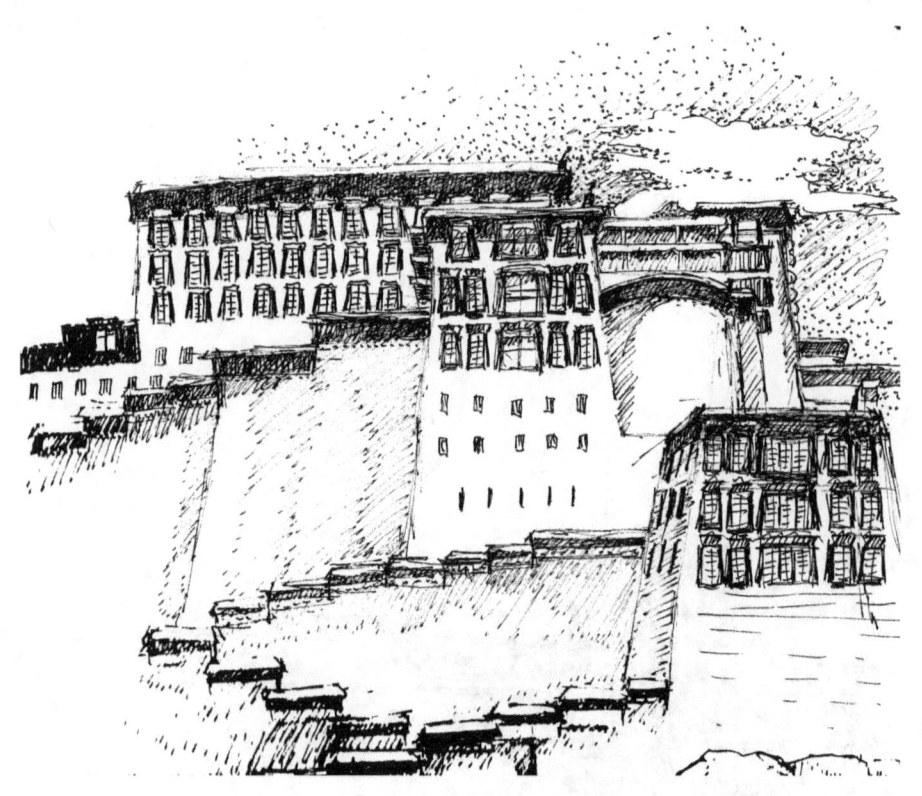

Tibet 1999

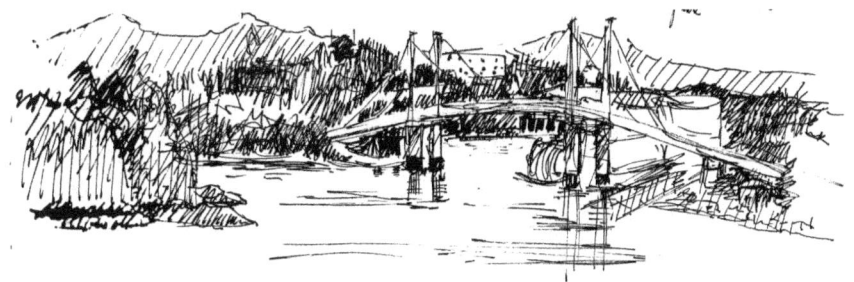

Sitka, Alaska 2004

My Dad

He carried me up those steep stairs,

    So scary, but he was safe.

He giggled at the antics of Tom and Jerry,

    But baseball was business.

He never swore or drank, was modest

    Cut his bacon with a knife and fork,

    But his smile was sweet in his eyes.

He had time, after retirement, for me,

    He worked to fulfill his mom's dreams

    And to repudiate his father's.

I lost him, then found him, lost him again

    In disease disorder.

Even so, he still carries me safely up those stairs.

        Nokomis, Florida 2016

Hatefulness, Hatefulness

On the road north to South Bend,

       Radio softly playing in the

       Morning weekend.

The 1971 Conelrad announces,

       "Hatefulness, hatefulness,

       From Cheyanne mountain."

The world is ending, the announcer quivers.

We stop, seeking the roadside, debate:

       Go back, go back!

       Jan shouldn't die alone,

To die alone is hatefulness.

                  Nokomis   2016

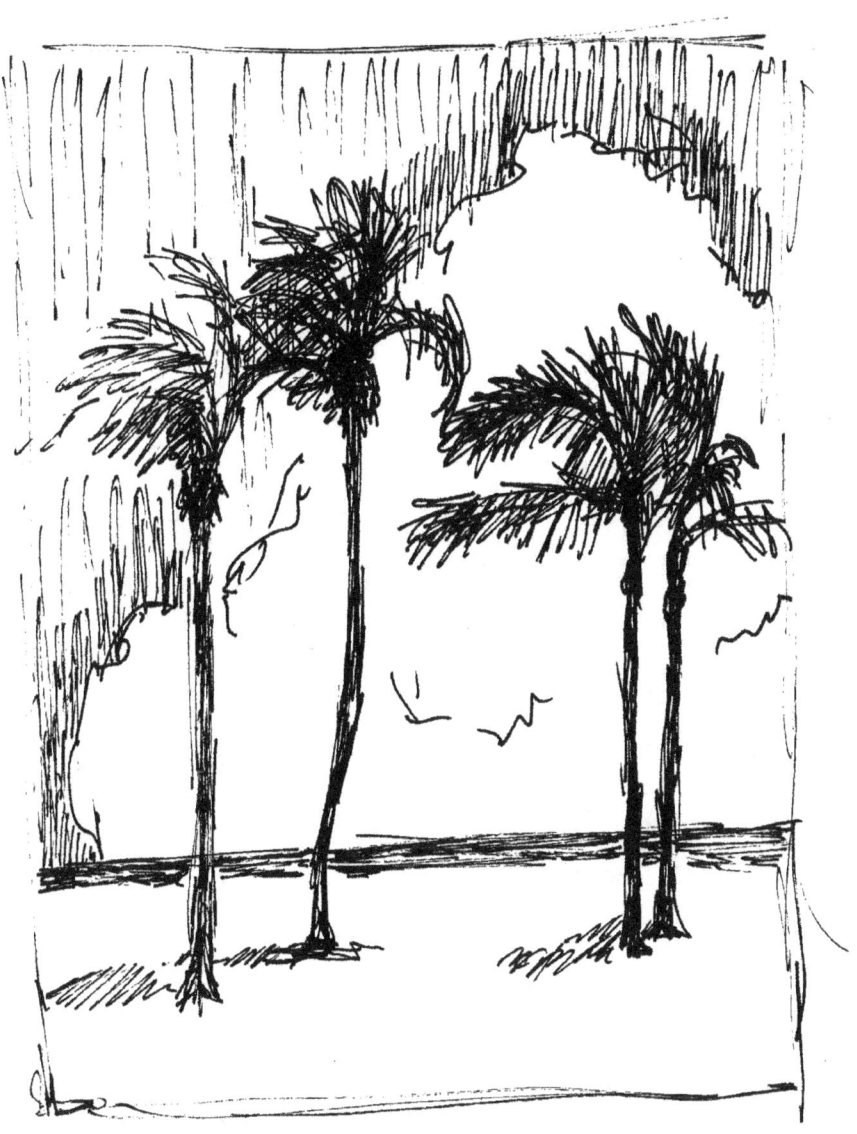

Florida 2015

Earth Rotation

The earth rotates slowly, holding us to itself,

Plates move inches quietly backing up,

      Moving markers,

Lava groans downhill, carving new vistas,

Stones simmer up from lowly graves

      To smile at sunlight,

Rivers cut away at stone banks,

      Grooving its direction to the sea,

Wind-blown sand drifts, blocking roads,

      Erasing footprints.

And I never felt a thing.

          Syracuse, Indiana 2009

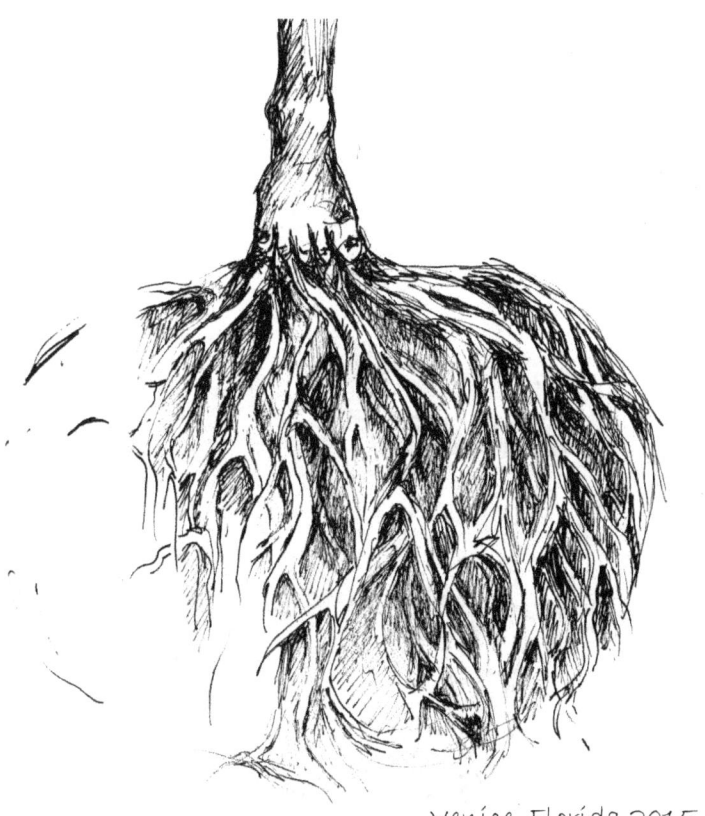

Venice, Florida 2015

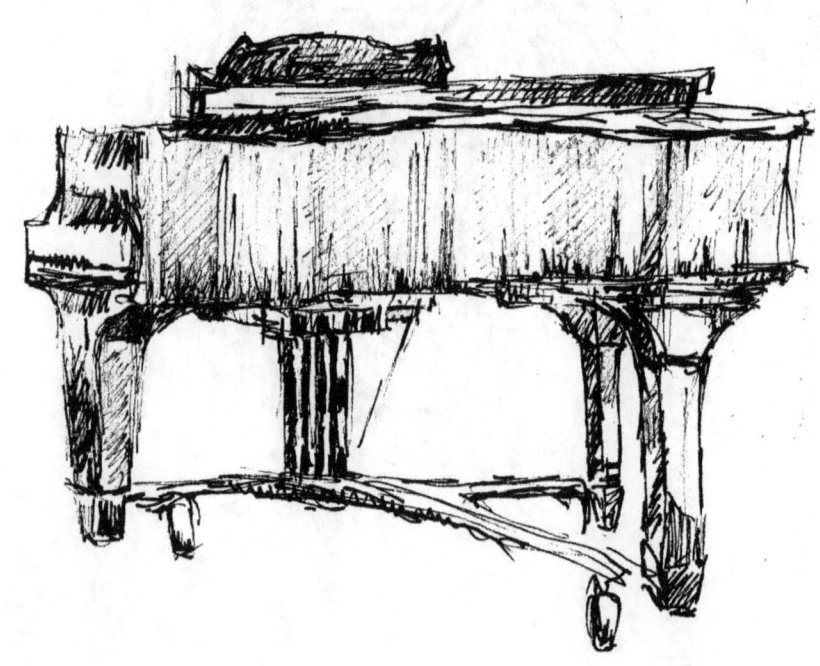

Venice, Florida 2016

The Proper Purpose of Art

In solemn splendor, fragments of
    Golden glass
March with covered hands
    Bringing tribute in
    Covert ceremony through
    Glass cubes.
Scene of secret sacrament
    Selects an uncommon miracle
As the symbol and token of
    Abiding power.
In strict frontal view as
    Certain children's drawing,
Mixing stones of differing shades,
    Both primitive and sophisticated,
    With clarity of representation,
Christ will feed and that is
    Useful in the telling.

Nokomis, Florida 2016

About the Author

Artist and author, Sara Robbins, grew up in Westfield and Carmel, Indiana.

She was an art area major at Ball State University, received a M.S. degree in Art Education from Indiana University, Fort Wayne and Indianapolis, taught secondary art for over 28 years, has been married for 49 years and has two children and four grandchildren.

Sara has traveled extensively both in the states and abroad, has attended innumerable workshops, has studied under several professional artists, has exhibited at galleries, art centers, art fairs and private shows.

After retiring in Florida, she continues to make art, especially drawing, painting in oils and watercolors, visual journals and printmaking. Writing poetry was her, up-to-now, secret passion.

Favorite quote: "How we spend our days is, of course, how we spend our lives." Annie Dillard

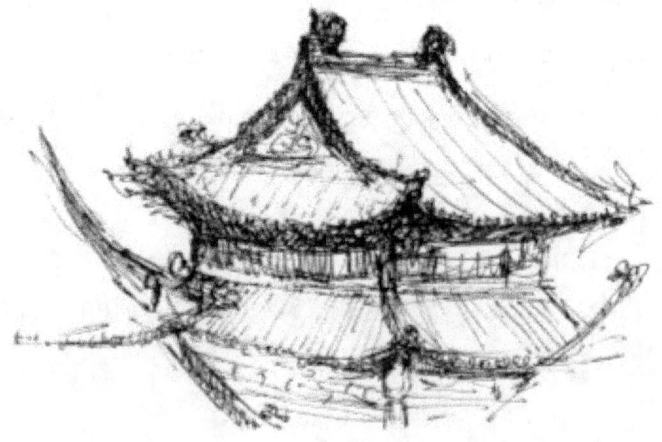

Beijing, China 1999

Robbins Books

Locks of Lollipops by Kristin Steffen & Sara Robbins

An illustrated children's book.

Three Goals by Mason Robbins

Peace Corps experiences in Haiti.

Touching Stones by Sara Robbins

Poems and sketches.

Appalachian Tales by Joel Robbins

Fiction: Walking the Appalachian Trail.

Ersatz News by Joel & Mason Robbins

News you'll want to read?

InGear by Joel Robbins

Peace Corps experiences and Hoosier humor.

Ursa Caucasia by Joel Robbins

Fiction: Traveling in Central Asia.

Welsh Pears by Joel Robbins

Fiction: A quest for love and meaning.

www.ingramcontent.com/pod-product-compliance
Lightning Source LLC
Chambersburg PA
CBHW070401190526
45169CB00003B/1059